The Nazi Economic Recovery 1932 – 1938

Prepared for
The Economic History Society by

R. J. OVERY
King's College, London

MACMILLAN

First published 1982
Reprinted 1984, 1989, 1990 (twice)

Published by
MACMILLAN EDUCATION LTD
Houndmills, Basingstoke, Hampshire RG21 2XS
and London
Companies and representatives
throughout the world

Printed in Hong Kong

ISBN 0–333–31119–1

S

T

F

c

been made of in

Originally entitled 'Studies in Economic History', series had its scope extended to include topics in social history and the new series title, 'Studies in Economic and Social History' signalises this development.

The series gives readers access to the best work done, helps them to draw their own conclusions in major fields of study, and by means of the critical bibliography in each book guides them in the selection of further reading. The aim is to provide a springboard to further work rather than a set of pre-packaged conclusions or short-cuts.

ECONOMIC HISTORY SOCIETY

The Economic History Society, which numbers around 3000 members, publishes the *Economic History Review* four times a year (free to members) and holds an annual conference. Enquiries about membership should be addressed to the Assistant Secretary, Economic History Society, PO Box 190, 1 Greville Road, Cambridge CB1 3QG. Full-time students may join at special rates.

STUDIES IN ECONOMIC AND SOCIAL HISTORY

Edited for the Economic History Society by L.A. Clarkson

PUBLISHED

W.I. *Albert* Latin America and the World Economy from Independence to 1930
B.W.E. *Alford* British Economic Performance since 1945
B.W.E. *Alford* Depression and Recovery? British Economic Growth, 1918–1939
Michael Anderson Approaches to the History of the Western Family, 1500–1914
P.J. *Cain* Economic Foundations of British Overseas Expansion, 1815–1914
S.D. *Chapman* The Cotton Industry in the Industrial Revolution
Neil Charlesworth British Rule and the Indian Economy, 1800–1914
R.A. *Church* The Great Victorian Boom, 1850–1873
L.A. *Clarkson* Proto-Industrialization: The First Phase of Industrialization?
D.C. *Coleman* Industry in Tudor and Stuart England
P.L. *Cottrell* British Overseas Investment in the Nineteenth Century
M.A. *Crowther* Social Policy in Britain, 1914–1939
Ian M. *Drummond* The Gold Standard and the International Monetary System, 1900–1939
M.E. *Falkus* The Industrialisation of Russia, 1700–1914
Peter *Fearon* The Origins and Nature of the Great Slump, 1929–1932
T.R. *Gourvish* Railways and the British Economy, 1830–1914
Robert *Gray* The Aristocracy of Labour in Nineteenth-century Britain *c.* 1850–1900
J.R. *Harris* The British Iron Industry, 1700–1850
John *Hatcher* Plague, Population and the English Economy, 1348–1530
J.R. *Hay* The Origins of the Liberal Welfare Reforms, 1906–1914
R.H. *Hilton* The Decline of Serfdom in Medieval England
E.L. *Jones* The Development of English Agriculture, 1815–1973
John *Lovell* British Trade Unions, 1875–1933
W.J. *Macpherson* The Economic Development of Japan, *c.* 1868–1941
Donald N. *McCloskey* Econometric History
Hugh *Mcleod* Religion and the Working Class in Nineteenth-Century Britain
J.D. *Marshall* The Old Poor Law, 1795–1834
Alan S. *Milward* The Economic Effects of the Two World Wars on Britain
G.E. *Mingay* Enclosure and the Small Farmer in the Age of the Industrial Revolution
R.J. *Morris* Class and Class Consciousness in the Industrial Revolution, 1780–1850
J. Forbes *Munro* Britain in Tropical Africa, 1870–1960
A.E. *Musson* British Trade Unions, 1800–1875
Cormac Ó *Gráda* The Great Irish Famine
R.B. *Outhwaite* Inflation in Tudor and Early Stuart England
R.J. *Overy* The Nazi Economic Recovery, 1932–1938
P.L. *Payne* British Entrepreneurship in the Nineteenth Century
Roy *Porter* Disease, Medicine and Society in England, 1550–1860
Richard *Rodger* Nineteenth-century Housing, 1780–1914
Michael E. *Rose* The Relief of Poverty, 1834–1914
Michael *Sanderson* Education, Economic Change and Society in England, 1780–1870
S.B. *Saul* The Myth of the Great Depression, 1873–1896
Arthur J. *Taylor* Laissez-faire and State Intervention in Nineteenth-century Britain
Peter *Temin* Causal Factors in American Economic Growth in the Nineteenth Century
Joan *Thirsk* England's Agricultural Regions and Agrarian History, 1500–1750
Michael *Turner* Enclosures in Britain, 1750–1830
J.R. *Ward* Poverty and Progress in the Caribbean, 1800–1960

OTHER TITLES ARE IN PREPARATION

Contents

Acknowledgements

I would like to thank the following for encouragement, advice and discussion: Professor D. Coleman, H. James, Professor T. C. Smout, N. Stone, Professor A. Teichova. I should also like to express a general acknowledgement to all those authors, particularly in Germany, whose work has contributed to the writing of this pamphlet but which cannot be adequately acknowledged in a study without footnotes. For any misrepresentation that may have arisen in the course of writing so condensed an account, my apologies.

Note on References

References in the text within square brackets relate to the numbered items in the Bibliography, followed, where necessary, by the page numbers in italics, for example [1: *1--10*].

Editor's Preface

SINCE 1968, when the Economic History Society and Macmillan published the first of the 'Studies in Economic and Social History', the series has established itself as a major teaching tool in universities, colleges and schools, and as a familiar landmark in serious bookshops throughout the country. A great deal of the credit for this must go to the wise leadership of its first editor, Professor M. W. Flinn, who retired at the end of 1977. The books tend to be bigger now than they were originally, and inevitably more expensive; but they have continued to provide information in modest compass at a reasonable price by the standards of modern academic publications.

There is no intention of departing from the principles of the first decade. Each book aims to survey findings and discussion in an important field of economic or social history that has been the subject of recent lively debate. It is meant as an introduction for readers who are not themselves professional researchers but who want to know what the discussion is all about – students, teachers and others generally interested in the subject. The authors, rather than either taking a strongly partisan line or suppressing their own critical faculties, set out the arguments and the problems as fairly as they can, and attempt a critical summary and explanation of them from their own judgement. The discipline now embraces so wide a field in the study of the human past that it would be inappropriate for each book to follow an identical plan, but all volumes will normally contain an extensive descriptive bibliography.

The series is not meant to provide all the answers but to help readers to see the problems clearly enough to form their own conclusions. We shall never agree in history, but the discipline will be well served if we know what we are disagreeing about, and why.

T. C. SMOUT
Editor

University of St Andrews

1 Introduction: Some Perspectives

THE story of the German economy between 1929 and 1938 is a critical one in the history of modern Germany. Historians and economists still debate the issues of the depression, hoping to show that different economic policies might have stopped Hitler. The economic recovery itself raised important questions at the time about government and economic policy, and the discussion of why and how it happened has continued since 1945. Moreover the economic recovery lies at the centre of the 'positive' view of Hitler's Reich. If there is still deep disagreement about how the Nazi economy should be interpreted, there is general agreement that recovery did occur at a faster rate and to a higher level than almost anywhere else in Europe. Since the central feature of the recovery was the Nazis' willingness to undertake schemes of deficit-financing, the myth has taken root that Hitler was a Keynesian before Keynes, and being so won widespread support inside Germany in the years of peace and returning prosperity.

While there is some truth in this picture, it is only a partial truth. The economic recovery needs to be placed in a wider perspective. Indeed the very term 'recovery' is in some sense misleading. The German economy was relatively stagnant in the inter-war years. Two short bursts of growth (1925–9 and 1937–9) were indistinguishable in an overall picture of slow growth, economic discontent and the painful adjustment to the changed and unhealthy climate of the inter-war world economy. There is no disputing the fact that the German economy recovered from the disastrous trough reached in business activity by 1932. But throughout the inter-war years the German economy failed to match the growth rates of the pre-1914 period or the high growth rates after 1950. Trade revived slowly in the 1920s and collapsed in the 1930s. Domestic demand responded sluggishly in both decades. Productivity improved significantly only with the short rationalisation drive of the mid-1920s; full employment in the 1930s paid the price of a slower and more uneven growth of productivity. Wages barely recovered to the real level of 1913. Table I sets out the

9

longer-term growth record of the German economy. Moreover, Germany's economic performance compared less than favourably with that of the other major industrial powers, including Mussolini's

Table I

Annual Average Growth Rates in Germany of Selected Economic Indices 1870/1913–1950/70

	1870/1913	1913/50	1913/38	1950/60	1950/70
Growth of total production	2.9	1.2	2.6	7.6	6.2
Growth of output per capita	1.8	0.4	–	6.5	5.3
Growth of output per man-hour	2.1	0.9	1.3	6.0	5.0
Growth of exports (volume)	11.0	– 2.4	– 1.6	16.0	12.8
Fixed investment as % of GNP (excl. housing)	15.6*	–	9.7*	16.1	17.7

*Figures for 1900/13 and 1920/38.

Italy. Some international comparisons are set out in Table II. The economic miracle was very much a product of the post-Nazi era, not of the 1930s.

Historians have been too tempted to see the 1930s from a short-term perspective, giving it a prominence it does not quite deserve. In the same way, they have tried to explain the German revival in terms of a set of unorthodox 'fascist' economic policies, cutting it off from its historical and international context. Here again the Nazi economy must be put in perspective. Many of the policies, including 'work-creation' projects, control of foreign exchange, government intervention in banking and agricultural protection, were the products of the Weimar period and were not uniquely Nazi policies at all. The German economy had always enjoyed a higher degree of state involvement than the more liberal western economies. Under

Table II

Comparative Economic Performance of Selected Countries 1913–1937/8
(1913 = 100)

	GNP (1937)	Ind. Output (1937/8)	Output per man-hour (1938)	Real wages	Annual rate of growth*
USA	171.9	164	208	153	2.9%
Sweden	174.0	231	143	150	2.2%
Italy	154.2	196	165	n.a.	1.3%
UK	146.5	139	167	133	1.7%
Germany	136.4	144	137	109	1.2%
France	120.8	119	178	128	0.7%

* 1913-50.

the impact of the defeat of 1918, the inflation and the 1929 crash this involvement became more respectable and widespread. Hitler's economic and business policies for recovery were not fascist in themselves. Many such policies have been pursued in more subtle and less brutal ways by the countries of the EEC. The same is true of the more general structural changes in the German economy during the period. Policies to revive heavy industry more quickly than consumer industries, the regulation of trade, control over currency and credit could be found in the anti-depression armoury of other western powers, and were the product of the general weakness of the world economy, the poor state of European agriculture and widespread investment-shyness.

Why then should the German recovery have occasioned so much debate? One reason is the perennial desire to understand the workings of the business cycle, a need reaffirmed by the uneven growth performance of the western economy since the early 1970s. The German ·depression was more severe and recovery more pronounced than elsewhere, making this episode an important one for economist and historian alike. Another, and more serious, explanation lies in the link between economic performance and radical politics in inter-war Germany. The depression was inextricably linked with the course of German politics; economic policy was determined by narrowly political rather than economic circumstances. The rise of Nazism and its final consolidation of political power between 1933 and 1936 was bound up with the failure of the Weimar governments' economic strategy and with the recovery that

11

followed. Questions about the German inter-war economy turn into more general questions about the relationship between capitalism and politics, not only in Germany but in all advanced industrial economies.

To try to understand what this relationship was in Germany in the years between 1928 and 1938, historical discussion has centred around the causes of the German depression, the choices that were open to the Weimar governments in responding to it, and the precise way in which the Nazi government achieved recovery. While mindful of the wider perspectives, the following chapters are concerned to present the answers that historians have given to these narrower, but important, questions.

2   The German Economy from War to Depression

ON the eve of the first world war Germany possessed all the features of an advanced and expanding industrial economy. German trade was on the point of exceeding that of Great Britain. Output had increased at the rate of almost 3 per cent a year for forty years. German industry was highly competitive and was supported by a banking system and educational structure particularly favourable to industrial growth. Economic modernisation was reflected, too, in the changing social structure. Bismarck's Germany in 1871 had been predominantly rural; Germany in 1913 was predominantly, though by no means completely, industrial. The war did not reverse the direction of the German economy in any permanent way, but it did bring an abrupt halt to expansion. A combination of territorial losses, particularly of the industrial regions of Silesia, Lorraine and the Saar, together with the collapse of German trade and the shortage of capital, contributed to the decline in German industrial production in the years 1919 to 1924 to between a half and three-quarters of the level of 1913. To these difficulties were added those of the inflation, which reduced savings sharply and slowed down the expansion of demand in the post-war period.

Nevertheless the German economy did recover slowly during the 1920s towards the level of 1913. The revival of industrial output, though it lagged behind the rest of Europe and far behind that of the United States, did lead by 1928 to a restoration of the output and trade levels of the pre-war world. The revival was based largely on foreign investment to provide the resources which the German capital market lacked and the 'rationalisation' drive which the foreign credits helped to pay for. Between 1925 and 1929 output per man-hour in the major industries expanded by 17 per cent, while large new capacity was set up using the most modern production methods. Technological change, which had been slowed down by the impact of war, became once again an important engine for growth within the industrial core of the German economy [13; 27].

The recovery of the 1920s disguised many structural weaknesses. It

13

was a fragile recovery, restoring pre-war achievements but exhibiting few signs of sustained expansion and buoyant growth as in the years before 1914. Looked at in long-term perspective it is difficult to dispute Petzina's conclusion that the 1920s, or for that matter the whole inter-war period, was for Germany a period of economic stagnation. Where GNP doubled in Germany between 1890 and 1913 and tripled between 1950 and 1970 it increased by only 4 per cent between 1913 and 1929 [59: 10–74]. The causes of the low level of growth in the 1920s were many. The loss of important industrial regions under the terms of the peace settlement in 1919 was in itself a significant blow to Germany's economic recovery. But of more lasting significance were Germany's troubled relationship with the world market, and the related question of war reparations. Recent research has sought to emphasise that world conditions were much less important a factor than the Germans themselves believed in the Weimar period; but even in a broader economic or political context it is clear that Germany's economic problems were related in many ways to the general problems of the world economy.

The sluggish growth of world trade in the 1920s, and the worsening terms of trade for primary producers, hit the German economy particularly hard as it relied on a high export base to sustain growth. Germany's share of world exports fell 31 per cent between 1913 and 1927/9, even further than that of Britain. Germany's trade with primary producers fell by over a third over the same period. The general shortage of capital on the world market had the same effect on German trade, since it reduced demand for German goods in third markets which had been financed before the war by French or British capital exports. Against the background of poorer trade was set the problem of reparations. War-related debts were an additional burden on the balance of payments, the more so as Germany's economy failed to expand as fast in the 1920s as her enemies had hoped. If it can be argued that Germans exaggerated the economic cost of reparations in the 1920s for political reasons, they cannot be ignored altogether. Moreover the reparations question helps to illustrate that underlying all these problems there existed the permanent danger during the 1920s that the structural weaknesses of the world monetary and payments system, exacerbated by unilateral protective and defensive policies, would undermine what efforts the German economy was actually making to expand activity and honour debts.

The impact of the world economy on Germany might well have been less damaging during the 1920s had there not also been signifi-

14

cant constraints within the domestic economy as well. One basic problem was the structure of the capital market in the post-war period. The war and inflation had reduced the funds available for investment and kept interest rates high throughout the 1920s. Although such rates encouraged the import of capital to make good the domestic shortage, many smaller producers and farmers were left short of capital and there was a general failure to produce investment levels high enough to sustain a more rapid rise in income. Indeed the small farmer and small businessman became an increasing drag on the economy. The high growth rates of the pre-war years had disguised the survival of large numbers of smaller and less efficient producers. The unhappier economic climate of the 1920s exposed the social and structural imbalance of the German economy. German agriculture was unable to compete with more efficient farmers in Europe and elsewhere, was small in scale, and was concentrated, in some areas, on the wrong crops. The long-term decline in prices coupled with the growth of agricultural indebtedness – an increase from 4.6 billion marks in 1924 to 11.5 billion in 1929 – and higher taxes, reduced agricultural incomes and the demand for goods from the countryside. The deterioration of the terms of trade for primary products within Germany meant that farmers could buy fewer manu- factures with what they produced than before the war. Where manu- factured goods increased in price 57 per cent between 1913 and 1929, farm products increased by only 30 per cent [59: *107*]. Nor were there significant gains in agricultural productivity during the 1920s. Further mechanisation spread relatively slowly. The farming population, which had declined more or less continuously as a proportion of the employed population between 1850 and 1913, remained at the 1913 level of 35 per cent until 1933. The slow revival of domestic demand during the 1920s reflected the survival of a very large, and relatively poorer, section of the German community in the countryside [59: *104–6*].

Things were not much better among the small shopkeepers and craftsmen. Since they too constituted a significant proportion of the German population, some 13 per cent in 1925, and since this group, like the peasantry, was suffering from relative decline throughout the 1920s, the effect on the growth of aggregate demand in the economy as a whole was clear. The contrast between a low level of economic development among the smaller and marginal producers and the rapid and expensive rationalisation of large-scale industry was a very pronounced one in Weimar Germany, leading, as Bessel has demonstrated, to a significant difference in economic performance within and between the major regions of Germany [10]. Moreover the investment programmes of the mid-1920s in large-scale industry led not only to an increase in output and improvements in productivity, but to higher levels of technological unemployment throughout the recovery period, which further depressed demand, while having the effect of maintaining under-employment on the land [20: *265*]. Peasants' sons were unable to find jobs in the cities, where large numbers were already unemployed. Public spending provided one of the only ways out of the problem of the slow growth of demand, unemployment and incipient crisis. The bulk of building activity was carried out by public authorities, some 47 per cent in 1928. The construction industry, and the public-works projects initiated in the regions after 1926, helped to maintain business activity and stimulate demand as they were to do later under the Nazis, but at the price of drawing in large foreign loans during the 1925–9 period that left the German economy very vulnerable to shifts in the world economy [22: *54, 113*; 71: *197*].

The sluggish revival of demand both at home and abroad slowed down the development of newer industries in Germany. Where other major industrial countries were expanding the output of new consumer durables, the German economy remained much more committed to the goods that had been produced before 1914. The aircraft industry and modern armaments were restricted or prohibited under the terms of the Versailles Treaty. Car production failed to expand in Germany as it did elsewhere. The fact that so large a proportion of the population was still working in less productive sectors, and that middle-class savings had been emasculated by the inflation, contributed to the low level of economic growth in the ten years after the end of the war. By 1929 the American economy was 70 per cent larger than in 1913, the French economy 38 per cent larger, that of Germany only 4 per cent larger [59: *6*].

Almost all these factors played some part in the depression that hit Germany at the end of the 1920s. What weight to attach to each factor has been the subject of much recent research and argument. Most explanations depend on first answering the question: when did the depression begin in Germany? The question of why the depression was so severe once it had started is easier, though not much easier, because most commentators have accepted that the answer must lie in the collapse of international trade and liquidity during the 1929–31 period. The first question, on the timing of the depression, depends upon what criteria are used to determine the onset of the economic downswing. The argument about the timing is an argument about the relative weight to attach to domestic factors on the one hand and to the problem of foreign lending on the other. Was the depression in Germany caused by the withdrawal of foreign investments and the collapse of the American stock market in late 1929, or was the withdrawal a result of the downswing of business activity in Germany already evident by the middle of 1928? Or a result of both?

In any discussion of the depression the question of foreign lending is clearly crucial. Germany borrowed large sums of money during the 1920s, the bulk of it from the United States. The money was loaned on both long-term and short-term bases, but tended to be reloaned within Germany on a long-term basis, making it difficult to repay short-term lending should it suddenly be recalled. The extent of such borrowing and capital flows into and out of Germany are set out in Table III. Up to 1928 the bulk of foreign lending was long-term. In

Table III
German Balance of Payments 1927-32 (m. RM)

	1927	1928	1929	1930	1931	1932
Current a/c balance	− 4244	− 931	− 2469	− 601	1040	257
Net long-term lending	1703	1788	660	967	126	− 36
Net short-term lending	1779	1335	765	117	477	− 763
Other capital movements	310	1000	879	− 594	− 3496	286
Capital a/c balance	3792	4123	2304	490	− 2693	− 513

Source: C. R. Harris, *Germany's Foreign Indebtedness* (1935) pp. 112, 114 [83: 243].

1927 however there was a switch to more short-term lending, and it is to fluctuations in this short-term lending that the downswing of the German economy has generally been attributed. Falkus has maintained that the German economy depended on foreign lending to maintain a satisfactory level of credit, and that since so much of the lending passed through the German banks any reduction in capital supplies from abroad would have the effect of producing a credit squeeze, higher interest rates and a fall-off in business activity [24: *462–5*]. The evidence seems to suggest that foreign lending played just such a role. From the middle of 1928 onwards both short- and long-term lending slowed down, interest rates rose, imports of raw materials declined, industrial investment and employment levels began to fall. During 1929 the situation became worse, with net capital imports falling from 4.3 billion marks in 1928 to only 2.7 billion in 1929. The outflow of funds was caused partly by the greater attraction of American sources of investment, and partly by German investors trying to find a safer home abroad for their capital because of the signs that the German economy was entering a period of slow or declining growth and was a less secure, and less profitable, proposition than in 1927 and 1928.

It is over this very question that the role of foreign lending becomes far less clear-cut. If Germany was a less attractive investment prospect in 1928 it is easy to see why. The structural problems already discussed, the slow revival of consumer demand, the crisis in agriculture, the slow expansion of trade and the problem of reparations had all contributed to the fragility of the German recovery. The price of German industrial shares declined from a peak reached as early as April 1927. Industrial investment began to turn down in 1928, inventory investment fell by 1.7 billion marks in the same year, unemployment began to rise from mid-1928 and had already reached 2.8 million by March 1929. It is tempting to see this slow march into depression (so different from the dramatic and sudden collapse in the United States) as Temin and Borchardt have seen it, as the result of a demand crisis in Germany that discouraged businessmen from a continued course of expansion in 1928 [11: *3–6*; 88: *246-8*]. There is certainly evidence that demand was slackening off well before the reduction in levels of foreign lending. The output of consumer goods of elastic demand, the durables that were sustaining other economies, turned downwards as early as February 1928. Net agricultural income was lower in 1928 than 1927. Moreover a close examination of the loans floated in 1928 and 1929 shows that the bulk were directed towards local government in Germany or towards utility investment and that the demand for loans by major German businesses had already slackened off well before the absolute decline in foreign loans. Some historians have argued that this slackening off was due to high wage costs and a profit squeeze. Yet in a period of rapidly improving productivity in industry it seems more likely, as Weisbrod has pointed out, that the reasons lay in the high cost of capital and the low expansion of sales, the result of weaknesses in the Weimar economy and not of excessive wage claims [91: *248–9*]. Earnings in fact expanded much more slowly in Germany than among her major competitors.

It is difficult not to conclude under these circumstances that the depression in Germany was a result of both endogenous and exogenous factors, a fall in foreign lending and a deterioration of the balance of payments coinciding with a sharp slowing down of the expansion of the economy due to structural constraints on demand. If anything the balance of evidence suggests that the relative stagnation of the German economy in the 1920s, the rise in costs and the slow revival of demand at home and abroad produced a downswing in the economy some time before the decline in foreign lending became significant.

Once the depression had begun to bite in 1929, however, there was no question but that it was made very much worse by the peculiar relationship that Germany had established with the world capital market in the years 1925-9. In 1929, both before and after the Great Crash, funds flowed rapidly out of Germany, but were more than made up for by funds flowing in. In 1930 there was a very small balance in Germany's favour. In 1931 a large-scale net outflow of domestic and foreign funds produced a massive liquidity crisis at both a national and an international level. What might have been a 'normal' business-cycle downswing turned into an economic catastrophe because of the recall of short-term loans and the drying up of long-term lending [28: *55-8*]. Against such a background some of the more positive aspects of the depression such as the active balance of trade (achieved for the first time in 1931) and the rapid increase in real incomes for those in employment were of little consolation.

The depression between 1929 and 1932 was characterised by a sharp fall in prices, particularly of agricultural prices, very high levels of unemployment and business failure, a sharp and sustained fall in investment activity of all kinds and a fall in government spending faster than that of national income. The result was a large-scale collapse of industrial output and levels of foreign trade, and a sharp fall in income. The details of the depression are set out in Table IV.

The course of the depression and the reasons for its severity were determined to a large extent by the nature of its causes. On the one hand the fall-off in demand, both at home and abroad, produced a contraction of industrial investment and a lowering of prices. On the other the difficulties of the international financial system deepened

Table IV
The Depression in Germany 1928–32

	1928	1929	1930	1931	1932
GNP (bn RM)	89.5	89.7	83.9	70.4	57.6
National income (bn RM)	75.4	76.0	70.2	57.5	45.2
Industrial production (1928 = 100)	100.0	100.1	87.0	70.1	58.0
Exports (bn RM)	12.3	13.5	12.0	9.6	5.7
Imports (bn RM)	14.0	13.5	10.4	6.7	4.7
Unemployment (m.)	1.4	1.8	3.1	4.5	5.6

Source: [34: *31*].

the depression, making it a far more catastrophic event than might otherwise have been the case. The international economic crisis affected all the main industrial powers, but it affected Germany with a particular severity. The first reason for this was the sharp decline in lending to Germany already noted. Then there was the problem of the withdrawal of funds already loaned. This was a much more serious problem. In 1931, with the German economy showing no sign of revival and international confidence at a low ebb, the withdrawal of funds became a flood. By the end of 1931 over 6.5 billion marks had been withdrawn from Germany or sent out by German investors seeking greater security. This aspect of the crisis might have been much worse again if international action had not been taken to protect the weaker industrial economies.

The crisis at an international level came to a head in June and July 1931, triggered off by the international reaction to the German proposal for a customs union with Austria. Throughout June funds were hastily withdrawn from the German banks. The traditionally cautious attitude of the German banks had been undermined during the 1920s by the general availability of foreign money. By 1929 the ratio of capital to deposits, which had been 1:3 or 4 in 1914 was as high as 1:20 [85: *113*]. Almost 50 per cent of the deposits held by the beginning of the recession was foreign money. Under these circumstances any sudden withdrawal of funds would be disastrous both for the banks' own liquidity and for the balance of payments. As the foreign creditors increased demands for repayment in the middle of 1931, the banks began to call in loans, as far as they could, from the firms to whom the money had been lent. It was at this point that the other interested parties intervened. In the United States President Hoover announced on 20 June a moratorium on all international capital movements. Five days later a loan of 420 million marks was paid to Germany to cope with the emergency. But by then the crisis had already deepened too much. It made little difference that the French refused to ratify the moratorium until 6 July. In the wake of the collapse of the Austrian banking system the first large German bank, the *Darmstädter und Nationalbank*, collapsed on 13 July [85: *111-15*; 20: *266*].

The German government adopted two lines of approach to the financial collapse. The first had been to press from 1930 onwards for international co-operation in solving the economic crisis and a reduction in the level of protective tariffs and discriminatory regulations that had been established by other countries as a defence against the depression. The effect of these protectionist measures had been to accelerate the decline of world trade, to reduce demand for German goods abroad and hence to reduce Germany's ability to pay the war-related debts. Although German complaints received a sympathetic hearing, there was little positive international co-operation to restore the world market to health [36]. The other line of approach was to take over the banking system, at least for the duration of the crisis, and to try to control as far as possible the flows of capital, the foreign exchange market and the structure of internal credit. Compelled by necessity both the banks and the government co-operated to replace private banking and financial institutions with a system of public regulation and control.

The banking crisis elicited the first positive efforts on the part of the government, or private business for that matter, to alleviate the worst effects of the depression. And it was perhaps significant that such efforts were not made until the German economy seemed on the point of complete collapse. To many historians since the depression the actions of the German government throughout the crisis have had the appearance of shutting the stable door well after the horse has bolted. In the light of the fact that the crisis was so much more severe than earlier crises, there is a strong case for arguing that the German government, and particularly the government of Chancellor Brüning which took office in March 1930, should have used government powers to reduce the impact of the depression. Policies of lower interest rates, increased government expenditure (by deficit if necessary) and devaluation to make German exports more competitive have all been canvassed by economists and economic historians as policies that would have combated the crisis and perhaps have avoided the triumph of fascism in 1933.

The main problem with such an argument is that it takes little account of the historical circumstances with which the German government was faced. In the first place it was by no means clear until the sharp financial crisis of 1931 that the depression was any different from earlier depressions. The short downswing in 1926 had produced a level of industrial production and employment lower than that in Germany at the end of 1930. Borchardt has argued that there were signs of recovery in Germany and in the world economy in the early months of 1931 that would have suggested to any government at the time that the purging process of recession was over and extraordinary policies therefore unnecessary [11: 5–7]. In the second place the government and states in Germany already played an important part in the German economy before 1929 and there was widespread resistance in the private sector to the further extension of government intervention in the economy, as there was in Britain and France as well. The laissez-faire attitudes of many German businessmen and politicians were not a product of prejudice or self-interest alone, but were the product of a genuine belief that there was no other way to weather a recession but through traditional, deflationary means. To have done otherwise would have been to fly in the face of prevailing economic theory and political inclination.

Given these circumstances it is by no means clear that historians' remedies for the problems of the depression in Germany would have been recognised as necessary by contemporaries or would even have worked. Low interest rates were unlikely to have had the necessary effect since there were many other factors affecting entrepreneurial decisions in 1930–2. Moreover high interest rates were deemed necessary in a situation where German creditworthiness and international liquidity were high priorities. A higher level of government spending by itself would have alleviated some of the unemployment, but would have produced consternation among the conservative politicians and financiers abroad who were in a position to influence the course of German economic policy. Such a policy, if combined with devaluation of the mark, would have been regarded at the time as inflationary. In Germany the political effect of pursuing policies alleged to be inflationary would have been disastrous for Brüning. Nor was devaluation the answer. It would not necessarily have helped Germany's balance of trade (which was already in surplus by 1931) or balance of payments since it would have made payments more expensive and provided no guarantee that demand for German goods was likely to revive given the general nature of the trading and financial crisis. To have worked it would have required that other countries stopped devaluing competitively and reduced tariffs at the same time, which they were clearly unwilling to do. By contrast, a comparatively over-valued mark did have the advantage of making it progressively easier to pay off international debt and of reducing import prices, particularly of raw materials. In the political and economic context of the depression all policies carried advantages and disadvantages. There was no easy Keynesian answer to the crisis.

For the German government, faced with the uncertainties surrounding any less orthodox economic policy, it made much more sense to do as little as was necessary. The safe option that was chosen was deflation. This was the prevailing economic orthodoxy and it satisfied conservative political circles at home. It was the way almost all governments responded to economic crisis. There can be little doubt that this contributed, as did international economic problems, to deepening the recession. But it should not be exaggerated. In 1931 total budget expenditures fell from 13.1 billion marks in 1930 to 11.3 billion at current prices, a fall of 13 per cent. In real terms the fall was only 9.8 per cent. As a percentage of GNP government expenditure was actually higher in 1931 than in 1930. Even in 1932, with a sharper fall in the real value of government expenditure, the level was higher as a proportion of GNP than in any year of the 1920s. The deflation decrees, which began with the decree of 7 July 1930 by ordering a 10 per cent reduction of all wages, prices, rents and profits and continued throughout 1931 and 1932, were designed to have the positive effect of lowering variable costs for industry. High wages and artificially high cartel prices were cited by many businessmen as an explanation for declining profits and business crisis. The deflation was designed to lower these costs to compensate for the high cost of capital. The government also pursued other policies of a regulatory kind where necessary, particularly with the banks and the foreign exchanges, or palliative policies, not unlike those pursued in Britain, to divert extra funds to the more depressed regions and to encourage a limited number of public works.

What the government did not do was to introduce policies to stimulate demand or investment policies to increase national income, or not until compelled to do so by the changing political circumstances and the high level of unemployment at the end of 1932.

Stolper, among others, has suggested that expansionary or Keynesian policies were not pursued because no such alternatives were ever seriously proposed [85: *116–18*]. Chancellor Brüning appears as the typical pre-Keynesian politican. Yet this was not the case. There were alternative economic strategies available and some were widely canvassed at the time. Throughout 1931 and 1932 an active debate was carried on over the appropriate economic strategy for Germany to adopt. Opposed to the orthodox laissez-faire economists were those like Wilhelm Röpke whose reports for the Brauns-Commission in 1931 stressed the need for a 'first spark' (*Initialzündung*) in the form of government investment programmes to get industrial production going again [73: *430-5*]. Garvy has stressed that German economists were familiar by the 1920s with many of the ideas developed later in Keynes's *General Theory*. Books like those by Dräger on *Arbeitsbeschaffung durch produktive Kreditschöpfung* ('Work-creation through the productive creation of credit') and Wagemann on *Geld- und Kreditreform* ('Money and Credit Reform'), both published in 1932, could have provided the government with the theoretical basis for expansionary policies [30: *397-8*]. Efforts were even made to recruit Keynes to help to persuade the government to adopt a programme of public works, tax concessions and expanded industrial investment, but Keynes declined to help on the curious ground that his German was not good enough. The problem faced by those favouring unorthodox expansionary policies was their lack of political influence. This was not just because Brüning himself now seems to have been opposed to schemes of deficit-financing on theoretical grounds, but to the fact that the champions of a new economic theory were of junior rank or were outsiders like Röpke or Woytinsky with no political power base [84: *103-5*].

This fact throws into sharp relief the central answer to the question of why the German government failed to respond to the depression with Keynesian or quasi-Keynesian policies. The main factors governing policy-choice were not economic but political. Much recent research in Germany has been concentrated on showing how economic choices were governed by political pressures and constraints, particularly through domestic politics rather than foreign policy; *Innenpolitik* rather than *Aussenpolitik*, on which more traditional explanations have been based. Had the factors been simply economic it might have been possible to devise the necessary policies for economic revival. But they were not. Brüning's capacity for action during the depression was crucially governed by political questions.

In the first place, as Brüning himself has argued since, German policy was dependent on the attitude and actions of other powers. This is a point that needs to be re-emphasised; recent historians have been too ready to relegate it to the sidelines. Reparations required that Germany be seen to be behaving responsibly in economic affairs. So, too, did the high level of foreign debt that bound Germany much more than other powers to more scrupulous trade and financial policies. A high premium was placed upon confidence in Germany's creditworthiness as a precondition for any renegotiation of the Versailles settlement, a fact of increasing importance in 1929–31 with the growing strength of French finances and the possibility of retaliation against German default. Some of these arguments seem hard to sustain in the light of the Nazis' ability to ignore international agreements and financial arrangements at will, but nevertheless the evidence shows overwhelmingly that international political considerations governed a large part of German policy-making in the central years of the depression.

Of equal importance, however, were questions of domestic politics. In the first place all political parties were agreed on the need to defend the currency at all costs. Deflationary policies guaranteed that there would be no repeat of the disastrous inflation of 1923. The link in people's minds between unorthodox economic policies and inflationary crisis may well have been a false one, but it nevertheless acted as a major psychological constraint in any discussion of new ways to fight the crisis. It is significant that not even the German Social Democratic Party (SPD) or the trade unions were prepared to do anything that threatened to upset economic 'stability'. The SPD, rather like the British Labour Party, failed conspicuously to approach the depression with any positive proposals. On the one hand they were persuaded by Hilferding that Marxists should defend the currency as vigorously as anyone because of the threat that inflation represented to the ordinary working man; and on the other they argued that they should do nothing that undermined rising real wages. Since prices were falling faster than wages for those in employment, and since the bulk of SPD votes came from those still with jobs, the socialist leaders argued, with a remarkable degree of circularity, that they should do nothing that jeopardised the short-term gain in real income [94: 462-72]. This position, and that of the conservative parties, was strengthened by the unfortunate fact that unorthodox economic policy was associated with the political extremes, with the German Communist Party and the Nazis. Both parties, from different angles, stressed the need for state policies in combating unemployment, for cutting Germany off much more from the effects of the world market, for opposing deflationary and orthodox economic policies. In the political circumstances of 1931 and 1932 it seemed to many that to pursue expansionary economic policies was to lurch into radicalism.

This political division was complicated even more by what German historians have come to call interest-group politics [31, 82, 91]. It was not merely the parties but also – and to a much greater extent – large-scale business and agrarian organisations that were involved in policy-making. This dimension was more important in Germany than elsewhere in Europe because of the considerable degree of social power and political influence exercised by the cartel leaders and the larger landholders. The obvious feature of interest-group politics is that each group has different interests. Industry itself was roughly divided between the export sector and the heavy industrial groups. Agriculture, because of the increasing need for protection, came to identify more with the latter. The export sector wanted efforts to revive trade, international co-operation and cheap raw materials. Heavy industry and agriculture wanted a more closed economy, protection and guaranteed cartel and agricultural prices [1]. All were agreed that efforts should be made to reduce wage costs, while maintaining artificially high prices for food products and industrial raw materials. The divisions were not, of course, exclusive. There were large corporations engaged in export and primary production. There were smaller farmers who favoured cheaper fodder imports but restrictions on other imported food. But there was general agreement that the government should not embark on any policy in favour of one group at the expense of the rest. In the face of so many conflicting interests any government had to tread warily. Brüning hoped to strike the right balance between interest groups, parties and foreign creditors by adopting the economic policy that divided them least. In the deepening recession of the winter of 1931–2, with the prospect of a settlement of war debts getting closer, the government determined to do nothing but hang on in the grim expectation of improvement. In May 1932 the German Minister of Labour announced gloomily that there seemed 'no possibility whereby the political authorities might overcome the existing difficulties' [84: *106*]. The Brüning government lacked the political imagination to overcome the purely political constraints, and was able to use such constraints as a justification for economic timidity. Yet given the way in which economic and political life was structured during the depression, it is difficult, in the end, to see how Brüning could have behaved otherwise. The strength of the interest groups he faced was amply demonstrated by the fact that the leading agrarian political circles were able to bring pressure to bear on President Hindenburg to dismiss Brüning in May 1932 because of his unfavourable attitude to the large aristocratic estates.

The irony of Brüning's dismissal was that circumstances were on the point of a sudden change. Even though reparations formed only a part of the problem, the outcome of the Lausanne Conference in June 1932 was a victory for the German government's painstaking efforts to reduce the burden of war debt in Germany. Secondly, as the orthodox economists had expected, the depression began to show signs of coming to an end in the summer of 1932. The output of producer's goods had turned up in the second quarter of 1932, that of consumer durables in the third quarter. Profits began to rise as a proportion of industrial income, while costs were beginning to fall far enough to restore some measure of business confidence. A more important change was in the prevailing attitude to government intervention. While many businessmen continued to resist pressure for more government intervention, the very intensity of the crisis, and the mounting fear of political extremism, inclined both politicians and businessmen to accept more state initiative in helping the economy to recover. Even the Brüning government had drawn up preliminary plans for work-creation projects [40: 232–4]. Armed with such preparations, and in the knowledge that economic conditions had now reached their lowest ebb, circumstances were ripe for some departure from the negative policies of the depression years. How great a departure continued to depend upon political circumstances.

3 *The Nature of the Recovery*

THERE is no general agreement about when the economic recovery began in Germany. Some indices show an early upward movement in the middle of 1932, but unemployment peaked slightly later and in the early months of 1933 there was a growing fear that the optimistic signs of the previous year, like those of 1931, had been a mirage. The *Institut für Konjunkturforschung* compared the period with the prolonged depression of 1875–95. Only by the second quarter of 1933 did it become clear that a more general improvement was taking place. By the end of that year the index of industrial production (1928 = 100) stood at 66, seven points higher than in 1932, and unemployment fell by over two million between March 1933 and March 1934. By 1935 GNP in real terms had reached the level of 1928. The peak figure of the 1920s for industrial production was reached by 1936, that for employment by 1937. By 1938 the economy was entering a period of growth well above the level of 1913 for the first time since the end of the war. The figures were not all that remarkable by international standards. Maddison has shown that almost all Germany's neighbours and major competitors had a higher growth record between 1913 and 1938 [52: *138–48*]. But the recovery was remarkable given the particular circumstances of the German economy at the beginning of the 1930s. A combination of structural problems and political instability made it seem likely to many contemporaries that the German economy would not be able to revive at all except through a lengthy and painful economic cleansing process. In fact the German economy grew at a faster rate during the 1930s than the world economy as a whole in the attempt to 'catch up' with the level of growth achieved elsewhere before 1929. The record of the recovery is set out in Table v.

There have been many explanations for this recovery. Some have centred on one particular factor – work-creation schemes or rearmament are among the favourites – but as more research is done it has become clear that there is no single or simple answer. At one level, indeed, it is possible to argue that the recovery was part of the

Table V
Statistics of Recovery in Germany 1932-8

	1928	1932	1933	1934	1935	1936	1937	1938
GNP (bn RM)	89.5	57.6	59.1	66.5	74.4	82.6	93.2	104.5
GNP (1928 prices)	89.5	71.9	73.7	83.7	92.3	101.2	114.2	126.2
National income (bn RM)	75.4	45.2	46.5	52.8	59.1	65.8	73.8	82.1
Industrial production (1928 = 100)	100	58	66	83	96	107	117	122
Unemployment (m.)	1.4	5.6	4.8	2.7	2.2	1.6	0.9	0.4

Source: [34: *277*].

normal business cycle. This was certainly the case in its early stages, before government policies began to make their effect felt. The necessity for restocking, the increasing attractiveness of restarting production with cheaper labour and raw materials and the solution of the international question in 1932 provided sufficient grounds for some sort of revival in business activity. How much weight to attach to the usual pattern of revival and how much to government efforts for expansion is difficult to say; but it is important to remember that it was not all a result of Nazi initiatives after 1933.

Part of the explanation lies with the changing relationship of the German economy to the rest of the world. The end of reparations in 1932 and the cessation of foreign lending removed two essentially destabilising elements from the German economy. The general move towards protection allowed Germany to isolate the economy from the normal operation of the world market and to avoid a repetition of the relationship established with the victor powers in the 1920s. But there was a price to pay for this change. German trade, like world trade, collapsed during the slump, exports falling by 1933 to 39 per cent of the level of 1928. This situation improved very little during the 1930s. The continued improvement in the German terms of trade, the relatively high value of the mark and the general crisis in world trade gave little opportunity for an export-led revival. The rise of protectionism in those markets which Germany had depended upon before 1929 merely confirmed the trends towards self-sufficiency, or autarky, apparent throughout the depression. Germany responded in kind by devising a system of controls over foreign trade and foreign exchange – Schacht's New Plan of 1934 – in order to guarantee the survival of any trade at all and to ensure the importing of vital foodstuffs and raw materials. Trade was carried on in some areas through bilateral agreements which by 1938 covered over 50 per cent of Germany's trade transactions.

Some of this trade went to south-east and central Europe, which many regarded as a natural outlet for German trade expansion. But there were limits even to Balkan trade, as recent research has pointed out. Contemporaries greatly exaggerated the importance of eastern Europe for the German economy. Kaiser has argued that eastern Europe was itself industrialising in the 1930s with the help of western capital and did not want to be drawn into a permanent, semi-colonial relationship with Germany [41: 141–2]. Indeed throughout the 1930s the Balkan countries fought shy of too close a link, leaving Germany with trading deficits with almost all her Balkan neighbours for most of the period [61: 398–403]. German trade continued to be predominantly with western Europe and Latin America and the Middle East. The Balkans bought only 6.9 per cent of German exports in 1935 and even by 1938, under growing political pressure from Germany, this figure had only risen to 11 per cent. The figures for total German trade are set out in Table VI.

Table VI
German Trade Statistics 1928–38

	1928	1932	1933	1934	1935	1936	1937	1938
Exports (bn RM)	12.3	5.7	4.9	4.2	4.3	4.8	5.9	5.3
Imports (bn RM)	14.0	4.7	4.2	4.5	4.2	4.2	5.5	5.4
Balance of trade	– 1.7	1.0	0.7	– 0.3	0.1	0.6	0.4	– 0.1

Source: [59: 483].

There was another disadvantage in Germany's growing isolation from the world market. The full effect of the fall in world prices, particularly of foodstuffs and other raw materials, was not passed on to the German consumer as it was in other advanced economies. In other countries the motor for expansion in the 1930s was provided by cheap imports, a consequent rise in real income and a growing demand for home-produced manufactures. In response to this increased demand for industrial goods further gains were made in improving technology and organisation to meet the demand. The rise in productivity then stimulated further demand growth. In this way home demand provided the kind of stimulus that had been provided for many countries by the growth of trade before 1913 or 1929.

The question that immediately arises is where did the extra demand come from in Germany if not from abroad, or from large increases in real income produced by cheaper imports and food? Export growth had been vital to the Weimar economy; how was this gap to be made good in an economy where domestic demand had grown only slowly even in the buoyant years of the mid-1920s? The first thing to notice about the pattern of demand in the German economy after 1933 is the shift from demand for consumer goods to demand for capital goods and industrial raw materials. In other words the expansion of domestic demand did not depend so much on the growth of consumption, as it did in the 1920s, but more on the growth of heavy industry and construction. Table VII shows the

Table VII

Relative Growth of Producer and Consumer Goods in Germany 1929–38
(1928 = 100)

	1929	1932	1938
Total production	110.9	58.7	124.7
Capital goods	103.2	45.7	135.9
Consumer goods	98.5	78.1	107.8
Pig-iron	113.8	33.4	157.3
Machinery	103.8	40.7	147.7
Chemicals	91.8	50.9	127.0
Textiles	92.4	79.2	107.5
Household furniture	104.2	69.6	113.6

Source: [60: 352].

changing relationship between consumer-goods and capital-goods production between 1933 and 1938. The second important feature is the high level of government expenditure. The main explanation for increases in demand lies with the increase in public investment and policies designed directly or indirectly to stimulate demand. How much effect such policies had will be discussed in greater detail in

Chapter 4. Government policies, particularly for construction and rearmament expenditure, were also responsible for shifting the emphasis of growth from consumer industries to the other major sectors of the economy.

Some government policies, it is true, were designed to stimulate consumer spending as well. This was true of agricultural policy. Farquharson has shown that a feature of the late 1920s and the depression years was the decline of agricultural prices and the relative increase in taxation and debt charges for farmers. Some efforts were made in 1932 to improve the situation but not until the Nazis came to power, partly on the basis of the peasant vote, were measures promoted to increase prices for farmers by granting a guaranteed minimum price, and to reduce the burden of taxation and interest. These payments represented 22 per cent of the value of farm output in 1932. By 1934/5 they stood at 13 per cent. Agrarian incomes increased by 17 per cent in the first year of recovery, 16 per cent in the second, while incomes for all sectors of the economy expanded in those periods by only 6 per cent and 12 per cent. By 1934/5 the agricultural surplus was almost 50 per cent higher than it had been in 1928/9 [25: 66–7]. Farmers bought tractors and fertilisers with the new money, providing in turn a stimulus to the manufacturing sectors. It is difficult to estimate exactly what impact the increase in agricultural incomes had on the growth of demand, for some of the new income was used for saving and debt repayment; but it clearly was an important feature of the early years of recovery, and deserves more attention than it has received.

Demand was stimulated among small businessmen as well. Many had been hit particularly severely by the depression, with the aggregate income of small businesses declining from 20 billion marks in 1926 to only 11 billion by 1932. Government spending policies, directed once again in favour of a group sympathetic to the Nazi government, played an important part, whether through construction, rearmament or road-building, in providing contracts for small firms. There was a deliberate emphasis on encouraging small workshops to modernise by buying subsidised tools and equipment which in turn provided a further stimulus to the machinery and buiding materials industries. Other middle-class groups, many of whom had increased levels of savings by the mid-1930s compared with the post-inflation period, provided a source of demand for consumer durables such as cars, whose output trebled between 1933 and 1938. Finally demand increased, as in other advanced countries, through the continuous changes in the structure of the workforce away from low-paid, unskilled jobs to more skilled or white-collar employment, and through the significant shift from unemployment to re-employment, part cause, part effect, of the increase in demand.

However, there are serious objections to any demand-based analysis of the German recovery. Consumption and the consumer industries responded slowly to the general recovery, despite the fact that full employment was reached by 1937, and that the decline in foreign trade encouraged import substitution. Although Klein has argued that per-capita consumption reached the levels of 1929 by 1938, this achievement has to be set against an increase in real GNP per head of 31 per cent and of industrial output of 22 per cent over the level of 1929 [44: 11]. It is difficult not to agree with Balogh, writing in 1938, and with later critics, that the increase in consumer demand was well below the general increase in economic activity [7]. This is confirmed when looking at real wages for the period. It has already been shown that the fall in world prices was not passed on fully to the German consumer. Nor were changes in productivity, which were used instead to boost profits or to encourage higher investment. Expressed either as wage rates or as average earnings, the real value of incomes rose to a peak in 1930/1 and declined thereafter as Table VIII shows. Some account should also be taken of the deteriorating quality of goods and of increased taxation and other compulsory levies. The fact that taxation remained at a high level demonstrated that the government was anxious to restrict the increase in consumption. Far from pursuing Keynesian policies in the 1930s, the Nazi government controlled the growth of demand, actively intervening to restrain the increasing propensity to consume in the early years of recovery by redistributing income to those with a lower propensity to consume or by deliberately creating savings. Such policies reinforced the effect of debt repayment after 1933 observed by Svennilson which shifted much of the increased income away from those who might have spent it on more goods to those with a greater interest in taking up government loans [86: 39-51]. The government was then able to use the diverted money for its own purposes, particularly for the repayment of its own foreign debts and the preparation of the economy after 1936 for war.

The slow growth of domestic demand and the collapse of exports throws into sharp relief the importance of investment, and government investment in particular, in explaining the recovery. This was a

· Table VIII
Real Wages in Germany 1928–38

	Real wages (1913/14 = 100)	Money wages (1913/14 = 100)	Real earnings (1925/9 = 100)	Wages as % of NI	Private consumption as % of NI
1928	110	168	106	62	71
1930	122	180	114	–	–
1931	125	171	106	–	–
1932	120	144	91	64	83
1933	119	140	87	63	81
1934	116	140	88	62	76
1935	114	140	91	61	71
1936	112	140	93	59	64
1937	112	140	96	58	62
1938	112	141	101	57	59

Source: [15: 331, 362; 70: 438; 66: 438; 85: 150].

vital area, for it was the sharp fall in foreign investment, and subsequently of investment as a whole, that had created such havoc in the economy during the depression. The high rate of interest throughout the depression period and the poor financial position of the banks made it difficult and unattractive to acquire new funds. By 1931 large-scale disinvestment had set in in the private sector. By 1932 public investment fell to a third of the level of 1928. Most historians of the recovery have laid special emphasis, and rightly so, on the revival of investment as an explanation for the German recovery. In 1928 gross investment was 18 per cent of national income; by 1936 it was 26 per cent and by 1938 27.5 per cent.

Much of the new investment came from the state. Some 45 per cent of gross investment between 1933 and 1938 was paid for by government funds. This was the kind of strategy that many German economists had demanded in 1932 as the only way to combat unemployment and regenerate the economy. In fact the Nazi government went much further than expected in maintaining high levels of state expenditure and public investment throughout the 1930s. By 1938 state spending accounted for 33 per cent of GNP as against only 17 per cent in 1932. A large part of the later spending was directed towards war purposes and the building up of domestic synthetic production. It was financed in a number of different ways, partly through taxation (which remained at a high level throughout the period), partly through deficit-financing and a large increase in the government debt from 13.9 billion marks at the end of 1933 to 41.7 billion at the end of 1938. By 1938 the money supply was 70 per cent greater than in 1933, and 45 per cent greater than in 1929, the peak of the earlier revival [45: *135*]. To ensure that the money was spent in the way that they wanted, the Nazis instituted a complex system of controls over the money market and direct investment. As a result of these controls industry was compelled to maintain high levels of internal investment from undistributed profits. The freedom to issue shares for industrial expansion was effectively removed and all new share issues required government sanction. Private share issues had totalled 9 billion marks from 1926 to 1929. From 1933 to 1938 the figure was only 2.6 billion [22: *67*].

Private investment in general revived much more slowly than public. The incentives for different sectors were very uneven. On the one hand some of heavy industry, particularly iron and steel, suffered from over-capacity based on the large investment drive of the 1926–8 period. The problem here was not a lack of investment but how to utilise existing capacity. Other sectors in which investment was lacking were, on the other hand, discriminated against by government policy and were unable to get the capital needed. This particularly affected the export-orientated and consumer industries. Under such conflicting economic conditions it was difficult for private business confidence to be fully restored and, where private investment did occur in significant volume, it was in those sectors or industries, such as the motor industry, which the government had singled out for special concessions [64: *473–5*]. Under these circumstances public investment, or private investment under government control, came to play a key part in the expansion and restructuring of the domestic economy (see Table IX).

It might be expected that such a high level of investment, directed as much of it was by the state, would have produced an economy in

Table IX
Public and Private Investment in Germany 1928–38

	1928	1932	1933	1934	1935	1936	1937	1938
Total public investment (bn RM)	6.6	2.2	2.5	4.6	6.4	8.1	8.4	10.3
Total private investment (bn RM)	9.7	0.3	3.2	4.7	7.2	9.2	10.5	12.2
Total all investment (bn RM)	16.3	2.5	5.7	9.3	13.6	17.3	18.9	22.5
Private share issues (bn RM)	2.5	–	– 0.1	0.1	0.3	0.6	0.7	0.9
Net private industrial investment* (bn RM)	1.0	– 0.8	– 0.7	– 0.2	0.3	0.7	n.a.	n.a.
All net investment as a % of NI	9.3	– **	– **	5.3	8.8	11.5	13.1	15.7

Source: [22; *67*; 44: *255—6*; 50: *23, 38*].

* Excluding inventories. ** Negative net investment.

which the engine of growth was once again technological change. Landes and Svennilson both emphasise the importance of productivity growth and the 'new industries' for explaining what growth there was in the inter-war period [47, 86]. In the German case this would be a mistake. High investment levels did not lead to a corresponding increase in industrial productivity. Between 1929 and 1938 the average increase was 1.3 per cent, a quarter of the levels achieved in the 1950s. This was partly due to the labour-intensive nature of many of the revival policies, and partly to the absence of a sufficient pressure on firms to improve methods, in the form either of vigorous consumer demand or of higher profits, both of which were restricted by the state. Because of the nature of government controls and numerous government contracts, there was less incentive to be competitive or efficient. Firms that did make higher profits found themselves subject to special levies and taxes. Firms that produced a cheaper and more competitive product for the world market found themselves penalised by the system of controls on trade and the overvalued mark imposed by the government. Under these circumstances large gains in productivity, and any related increase in real income, were sacrificed to the government's determination to make the economy do what it wanted.

Public investment and spending policies of sufficiently large scale lay at the centre of the recovery and must remain the primary explanation, as they have been for a great many economic historians. There was not enough scope for export-led growth, or for growth based on the buoyant expansion of consumer demand, for both economic circumstances and government policy dictated otherwise. It was left to state expenditure to generate large increases in employment and income. How the money was disbursed and with what effect is the subject of the next chapter. But to be effective in the conditions of the early 1930s, state policy had to be directed not only towards investment but towards most of the variables at work in the economy. Increasingly the government was compelled to control prices, wages, private investment, the banks and all aspects of foreign trade. It was all these controls operating within the context of investment-led growth that helps to explain the scope and speed of the revival. The growth record should not, however, be exaggerated. Even by 1938 Germany was still catching up the ground that had been lost in the 1920s. Moreover there was a price to pay for government policy. The drive for autarky, the growth of state spending, the extension of controls, were all a by-product of the totalitarian political system. If

37

political instability and pressure-group politics provide an explanation for the problems of the depression, they disappeared in the 1933–8 period in the wake of the Nazi intention to stifle and oppress all opposition.

4   Government and Recovery

IF state action provides a central explanation for the recovery, it is also necessary to know which policies were the most important for growth and how they worked. On both of these questions there has been considerable disagreement, though all historians are agreed that the state did something to stimulate recovery.

There was nothing new about the state taking initiatives in the economy. Stolper has demonstrated that the decision to carry out anti-depression policies from the middle of 1932 was very much in the tradition of German state policy [85: *118–20*]. But it would be impossible to deny that the advent to power of Hitler's government in January 1933 did not represent an important shift away from the mixed liberal economy of the Weimar period. The Nazis approached the German economy with no definite plan, certainly nothing like the Soviet predictive planning of the 1930s. Instead the economy was made to fit into Hitler's political and ideological framework. The Nazis placed great emphasis on the need to solve unemployment as a guarantee for the political stability of the regime. If we cannot quite believe Hitler's claim to have spent sleepless nights trying to find a way to solve the question of 'Bread and Work', he clearly believed that he had been brought to power with a mandate to pursue a new economic course to get the German economy going again. For Hitler the fascist economy was to be controlled from above, like other areas of society, by a comprehensive system of regulations. Controls were established over trade, finance, investment, and over the less tangible aspects of the economy, the relations between state and business and between managers and labour. The long-term purpose was to create a buoyant economy with which to embark upon foreign policy initiatives designed to make all Germans into an economic 'master race'. In this way Hitler aimed to create a higher living standard for all Germans and to provide, by means of a vast new building programme, a material infrastructure that people would associate with the Thousand Year Reich [54, 89].

In order to achieve the economic recovery he wanted, Hitler was

39

prepared to give the responsibility for creating it to the bankers, civil servants and industrialists who had the expertise. It did not matter that the leading Nazis themselves knew very little about economics; what mattered was their ability to recruit and discipline those who did. The Nazis were also prepared (in fact they believed it to be an essential part of their economic strategy) to coerce any group or individual who stood in the way of their political and economic ambitions. 'The public interest before selfish interest' was the slogan used to justify the destruction of the labour organisations in May 1933, the aryanisation of Jewish businesses, and the harassment of individual businessmen like Hugo Junkers, who refused to produce warplanes for Göring and found his business nationalised. Even Schacht, Minister of Economics from 1934 to 1937 and responsible for much of the early recovery policy, was not indispensable and ended up in a concentration camp.

Because of this reliance on the existing expertise of business and civil service, it was unnecessary at first to create new institutions of economic management. The existing state structure was used for the purpose. Many of the controls and regulations instituted were, in turn, borrowed from previous regimes which had used them as instruments in an emergency. Indeed the Nazis fought shy of appearing to control the economy too closely in order not to alienate the business world too much. They expressed the hope that revival might be generated through private business initiative on the basis of a 'first spark' provided by the state. In fact, as Erbe argued in a Keynesian interpretation of the Nazi recovery published in 1958, private initiative did not respond vigorously and the 'first spark' turned, as Hitler had perhaps always intended, into a permanent involvement in the economy [22: 69]. It is essential to grasp the difference here between liberal recovery policies such as those in Britain and the United States which were designed to stimulate the early stages of a recovery which would then become self-sustaining and reduce the need for state intervention, and those of the Nazi regime. In Germany the economy travelled in the opposite direction, moving from a cautious introduction of state policies in 1933 to a complete system of controls – what Neumann called the 'command economy' – established by 1938 [62: 240–96]. The secret behind the Nazi economic revival was not merely proto-Keynesian spending policies but the whole 'package' of controls, all of them inter-dependent, all of them necessary to achieve what the Nazis wanted out of the economy. Without such a 'package' the economy might not have recovered to the extent that it did or in the way that Hitler's future war plans dictated. State intervention meant attacking the problems of the economy on a broad front and not at one particular point.

The central feature of Nazi policy was, nevertheless, a programme of government spending and public investment designed to stimulate demand and expand income. The strategy adopted had a number of different features. There were policies aimed at stimulating demand indirectly through increasing purchasing power and encouraging the propensity to consume of specific groups. This was done by a system of tax concessions and special grants. Tax levels were reduced for farmers, for small businesses and for heavy industry in the form of the remission of taxes already paid. The sums involved were not that great, and in the case of concessions to large-scale industry had much less effect than had been intended. The large firms used their new liquidity to repay bank debts rather than generate demand for goods and there was no guarantee that the banks would stimulate the economy with the new funds in quite the way intended [71: *256–8*]. The system of grants operated at the same time was more successful but again was of modest scope. Grants were given to newly-weds to spend on household goods and furniture, or to householders to encourage house-repair. Additional grants were given to industries to enable them to purchase machinery or to help towards the cost of hiring additional labour. Subsidies were also given for the re-employment or increased employment of domestic servants [50: *6–18*].

The indirect stimulus gave way during the course of 1933 and 1934 to a high level of direct state expenditure on industrial investment, construction and employment programmes. Indeed the indirect demand policies gave way by 1935 to policies designed to curb consumer spending in favour of higher investment activity and government-created demand. Public investment doubled between 1933 and 1934 and increased by almost 60 per cent again during 1935. In 1929 public investment was 35 per cent of gross investment; in 1935 it was 55 per cent. Total government expenditure increased in real terms by almost 300 per cent between 1933 and 1938, rising from 18 per cent to 33 per cent of GNP, as Table x shows. These were levels almost double those of the 1920s.

In addition to direct expenditure the government also sought to stimulate and control private investment activity in a number of different ways, to complement the efforts being made by the state. This control over the secondary and less direct results of government

41

Table x
Government Expenditure in Germany 1928–38 (bn RM)

	1928	1929	1932	1933	1934	1935	1936	1937	1938
Total expenditure (current prices)	11.7	12.4	8.6	9.4	12.8	13.9	15.8	19.3	29.3
Total expenditure (1900 prices)	6.6	6.9	6.3	7.1	9.4	10.0	11.1	13.4	20.4
as % of GNP	14.8	15.7	17.9	18.9	22.9	22.0	22.5	24.5	33.5

Source: [3: *245*].

activity was carried out not only to ensure that state money was not wasted but in order to divert private initiative into the areas that the state wanted, particularly into import substitution and rearmament. The stimulation of private investment was achieved first of all through the granting of contracts which required for their fulfilment a contribution from the individual firms and suppliers. The spin-off effect of placing such orders, whatever the product, increased in proportion with the growth in government expenditure. An exception was the armaments industry in which much of the basic investment and the running costs as well were provided by the state. Secondly, concessions were made to certain firms which promised to undertake expensive projects that fitted in with the government's wider policies. This was the only way in which the Nazis could induce I. G. Farben to continue synthetic oil and rubber production in the 1930s. Another device was the restriction of profits and dividends and the compulsory retention of funds within the firm for reinvestment. Lurie has shown that the reserves thus accumulated by business were more than enough to satisfy investment needs during the upswing, while the policy of tax concessions for firms acquiring new machinery or extending operations with the undistributed profits encouraged them to use the money to increase fixed capital [50: *124–7*]. The result of this mixture of carrot-and-stick policies was to push private investment by 1938 to levels above public investment and to maintain an overall high level of investment activity. But by 1938 war preparations had become much more important and much of the private investment was in effect paid for with government funds. To ensure that the private funds flowed where the Nazis wished, it became necessary to extend more and more formal control over the banking and capital structure so that by the end of the decade it was increasingly academic to talk of a private capital market.

The result of the spending policies was a sustained rise in national income and a sharp fall in unemployment. It can be seen from Table XI that the two indices moved in step with the increase in government

Table XI
National Income, Public Spending and Employment in Germany 1932-7
(1932 = 100)

	1933	1934	1935	1936	1937
National income	103.0	116.6	129.6	145.6	163.3
Public expenditure	109.3	148.8	161.6	183.7	224.4
Employment	104.0	120.0	127.0	136.0	146.0

Source: calculated from [3: *245*; 34: *277*; 44: *251*].

expenditure, with a lag to allow the increased credit to work through the system. It was Keynes who first publicised this link between government spending and an increase in income. Keynes argued that any increase in government spending would have the 'multiplier' effect of producing more income than the value of the initial expenditure because of the boost to demand and employment that it would generate. At a primary level it would encourage those who took government contracts to expand business, take on more workers and order more goods. Beyond the primary level were secondary effects as the newly employed workers spent their wages on goods; and so on. Economists debated in the 1930s what exactly the ratio of spending to income was. Keynes suggested that the ratio under average conditions was 1:2.5 or 3. In Nazi Germany the ratio was substantially lower. Erbe calculated a multiplier of 1.5 – an increase in government expenditure of 32.6 billion marks and an increase in income of 52.7 billion [22: *163*]. Given the very large sums of money spent by the government the increase in income was much lower than might have been expected. Bresciani-Turroni arrived at this conclusion in his work on the Nazi economy in the 1930s and it has been confirmed subsequently [14: *7–18*]. There are a number of possible explanations. One reason for the disappointing multiplier effect was the fact that private activity did not respond as expected and government money was simply a substitute for money that would otherwise have been generated through the private capital market, and not an addition. It was also due to the relatively poor productivity performance of the 1929–38 period (of which more later), as money was poured into the less productive areas of armaments, road-building and general construction. Both of these factors reflected the government's deliberate effort to encourage saving and discourage a higher propensity to consume, the reverse of Keynes's prescription.

Nevertheless if growth was not as high as it might have been, it was high enough to achieve what the government wanted: a regenerated economy and full employment. The employment effects of the policies were in some ways more dramatic and successful than the income effects. The government was particularly anxious that employment should be increased as rapidly as possible because it had come to power on the promise to provide 'Bread and Work'. In 1932 the first work-creation projects had been launched and were expanded during 1933. Some were more useful than others in absorbing labour and were soon eclipsed by the numbers absorbed back again into ordinary employment. In fact the most important areas for expanding employment were agriculture and the building industry, a fact that the American economist Baerwald had observed in 1934. In agriculture, reorganised and assisted from the start in 1933, unemployment fell from 238,000 in March 1933 to only 66,000 a year later. In the building industry the figures were 493,000 and 107,000 respectively. Among unskilled labourers, many of whom were absorbed into the general increase in business activity, the fall in unemployment was over half a million. These three groups between them accounted for 51 per cent of the decrease in unemployment between 1933 and 1934 [5: 621]. In addition the government sponsored schemes to increase re-employment of domestic servants and withdrew young Germans from the labour market through the compulsory Labour Service and, after 1935, through conscription. Here again it is clear that employment increased as a result of a number of policies working together, and not simply, or even primarily, through work-creation programmes, as the popular view of the Nazi economy would have it.

The novelty of the Nazi policies for expanding income and employment lay in the way in which they were financed. If the methods are commonplace today they were unorthodox by the standards of the 1930s and inclined many economists to criticise the government for the inflationary policies that it pursued. Historians since the war, armed with Keynesian theory and common sense, have seen that the danger of a serious inflation was remote in the years of recovery from 1932 to 1936 with the existence of large unused resources and strict government control over the financial markets.

The devices used were relatively simple. First and foremost the government undertook to increase the public debt. This was done, in the absence of foreign sources of funds, by borrowing on the capital market for long-term loans and by budget deficit-financing for short-term loans. The short-term financing of the deficit, that is the excess of government expenditure over government revenue, was done by issuing government bills. Much of the early financing was covered by these short-term work-creation bills, or rearmament 'Mefo'* bills which were used by the government contractors to pay for what they needed. The bills were then held by the banks, by the Reichsbank or by private investors and were to be repaid by the government after five years out of the anticipated increase in tax revenue. After 1935 the government increased the amount of long-term debt and consolidated some of the short-term, compelling financial institutions to take up the new treasury bills at a lower rate of interest and without the right of discount at the Reichsbank which the short-term bills had carried. The advantage of the early deficit-financing was that it encouraged a rapid increase in the liquidity of the system, for the bills could be used as a kind of currency. This reduced the dependence of industry on the banks, whose functions became increasingly limited during the 1930s, and increased the velocity of circulation. The pumping of additional funds into the economy was an essential way to overcome the restrictive character of the financial system and to unblock the channels of mercantile credit which had become slowed down or blocked by the collapse of 1931 and 1932.

Other forms of finance were more conventional. Tax revenues did indeed increase as Schacht had expected (in fact taxation was kept at very high levels throughout the 1930s), allowing the government to pay off both outstanding foreign debt and a large part of the debt contracted in the first years of recovery. The figures for government revenue, expenditure and debt are set out in Table XII. Private savings also expanded and were directed by the state into particular channels at the expense, as Poole shows, of private investment and consumption [71: 80]. From 1933 to 1936 private savings increased by 6.9 billion marks, almost all of which went into the savings banks and into Reich finance [34: 123]. By contrast private share issues, which relied on a higher level of private saving, fell from a peak of 2.5 billion marks in 1928 to an average of only 660 million marks for the years 1935–8. The bulk of all investible income after 1933 went

* Mefo = Metallurgische-Forschungsgesellschaft (a government holding company).

Table XII

Statistics on German Finance 1928/9–1938/9 (bn RM)*

	Government revenue	Government expenditure	Total debt	Money supply
1928/9	9.0	13.0	–	16.4
1932/3	6.6	9.2	12.3	13.4
1933/4	6.8	8.9	13.9	13.9
1934/5	8.2	12.6	15.9	15.7
1935/6	9.6	14.1	20.1	16.7
1936/7	11.4	17.3	25.8	18.1
1937/8	13.9	21.4	31.2	20.0
1938/9	17.7	32.9	41.7	23.7

* Fiscal year beginning 1 April for columns 1 and 2. End of fiscal year for column 3. End of calendar year for column 4.
Source: [3: *245*: 22: *54, 122*; 50: *36*].

towards financing state expenditures and not into the private capital market. As a result the banks increasingly became mere intermediaries, holding government stock and helping in the job of keeping bills circulating in the way that the government wanted. As in Italy the role of the traditional investment bank had been undermined by the financial crisis and replaced with investment directed largely by the state.

This discussion of how the recovery was financed begs the question of what the money was actually spent on. Implicit in this question is a further one: which of the areas of expenditure were the most important? To some extent both these questions are redundant. It has already been shown that government spending and public investment explain the strength and speed of the revival and it could be argued that what the money was spent on does not matter as long as it was spent. The reasons for asking more about these policies lies in the importance that many historians have attached to rearmament as the key explanation for the revival, a significance that has taken root in the popular perception of the Nazi economy. If the answer does indeed amount to rearmament, how did it generate economic growth? If not, what else was government money used for?

When Balogh was writing in the late 1930s or Erbe in the 1950s the answers seemed clear-cut. War preparation had been the intention of the government all along and war expenditures represented the bulk of government investment (over 50 per cent according to Erbe) [7: *461–5*; 22: *162–3*]. This was the chief factor in explaining growth over the period. More recent research has questioned this view, maintaining that the level of rearmament and war-related expenditures has been exaggerated. According to Milward rearmament was deliberately kept at a relatively low level because Hitler did not want to reduce civilian consumption too far and because, for the short 'Blitzkrieg' wars that the German army appeared to pursue, a limited armament was all that was necessary [57: *ch. I*]. In a sense both arguments are right, but not for the whole period. A detailed study of rearmament expenditure shows that it was much less important in the early years of recovery than the critics of the 1930s supposed. But it can also be shown that from 1936 onwards rearmament did assume a much greater significance, with a high level of expenditure, a general restructuring of the economy for waging war and the deliberate restraining of consumer expenditure.

The key years of recovery from 1932 to 1935 were years of relatively low military expenditure. From 1932/3 to 1934/5 the aggregate figure of secret budget expenditure for military purposes was 3.4 billion marks. To this should be added a figure of 2.1 billion for the special armaments bills with which the industrial investment necessary for rearmament was paid for [65: *119*]. Yet total central government expenditure over the same period was 31 billion marks. Rearmament represented some 17 per cent of total government expenditure, and only 1.3 per cent of GNP over the period. It is difficult to see, whatever its multiplier effects, how military expenditure on its own could have accounted for the recovery of business activity. In the later stages of recovery rearmament became much more important. Moreover the regime's explicit intention to prepare for war after 1936 meant that much of the revival of private activity was directed to rearmament purposes as well. But in the years before 1936 this was not the case, for private investment revived only slowly. In the armaments sector money came largely from the government and was not matched by a corresponding increase in private activity of the scale necessary to make armaments a leading sector. Nor did rearmament affect employment levels dramatically before 1935. Much of the early military expenditure was not on direct employment-creating schemes, and much of it was concentrated in high technology sectors which were more capital- than labour-intensive. There were technical 'spin-offs' to be had in the long run, but in terms of the recovery period itself the linkage effects generated by rearmament were perhaps less than those generated by other forms of government expenditure.

The same picture emerges if the argument shifts to the government's intention. The Nazi regime, while pledged in the long run to war and conquest, had other political and ideological irons in the fire. As we have already seen, a first priority was to restore employment levels and to initiate recovery in order to safeguard the political position of the regime. Hitler himself was absorbed in his fantastic plans for the rebuilding of German cities and the founding of new ones which called for a programme of construction on a vast scale [89]. The cities were to be linked up by the new fast motorways, the *Autobahnen*, on which work was started in 1934 and which fitted in with Hitler's programme of German motorisation, which he regarded as a racial and social necessity [64, 66]. Another major project was the completion of the electrification drive begun under the Weimar Republic. It was all such policies, pursued for pragmatic as well as ideological purposes, that contributed to the high level of government expenditure in the early years of the recovery. Rearmament formed only one part of the state's recovery drive.

The first of the key areas highlighted by the Nazis was work-creation. The policy was borrowed from, indeed had begun under, the von Papen and von Schleicher regimes of 1932. The purpose of the programmes was to create direct employment through government expenditure on labour-intensive schemes of repair, maintenance and construction. Total expenditure on the schemes from 1932 to the end of 1935 was just over five billion marks, or slightly under 1 per cent of GNP. The direct employment created by the schemes was calculated by Grebler at 990,000 by the end of 1934, excluding house-building. A further 750,000 were at work in the winter of 1933/4 on house-repair schemes paid for in part by the government [32: *513–6*]. The short-term employment effect of the schemes was thus to absorb a large proportion of those unemployed in the late part of 1933. But the other economic effects were less than might be expected. If some writers in the 1930s were impressed by the scheme of public works, there were many at the time, and since the war, who have been sceptical about their economic significance. The first problem, as with rearmament, was the scale of expenditure. The amounts expended in the first months were very modest. The amount of extra income generated by the 1.5 billions spent by the end of 1933 cannot be accurately discovered, but the total increase in national income between 1932 and 1933 was only 1.4 billions and could only have been raised further by very much larger amounts of government spending. Work-creation may well have been responsible for preventing business activity from declining to yet lower levels in 1932 and 1933, but it is doubtful if it provided a sufficient boost to the economy to explain the strength and speed of the revival.

The industrial strategy of the Nazis was more successful in terms of generating growth because of the linkage effects it produced and the stimulus it offered to particular areas of private business. Of the major industries affected most authors have stressed construction as the key growth area [71: *210-11*]. Other research has emphasised the role played by *Motorisierung*, the policy designed to speed up the application of the motor vehicle to the German economy [64, 66]. In the case of motorisation the strategy was based not only on the vehicle industry itself, but on all the associated infrastructure, and particularly on the roads. At this point the boosts for both construction and the motor industry coincide and it is difficult, and unnecessary, to separate them. What is clear is that through a number of policies of tax concessions, subsidy and direct investment both sectors were able to grow very much faster than the economy as a whole, and to drag a significant section of the rest of the industrial economy along with them. Car production was almost 50 per cent higher in 1934 than the peak reached in 1929; expenditure on the roads (local and national) was 100 per cent higher in 1934 than in the peak year of the 1920s. The years 1932-7 were the years when the motorisation of Germany caught up with the levels achieved in other countries considerably earlier. A combination of government encouragement through propaganda and fiscal policy, increased agricultural prosperity (which encouraged farmers to buy vehicles) and a growing propensity among middle-class Germans to spend some of their growing savings on motor-cars, accounted for the buoyant growth of this particular sector.

The construction industry was similarly helped by government concessions and a high level of direct investment. Like the motor sector, construction grew more quickly than the economy as a whole. New construction totalled 2 billion marks in value in 1932. By 1934 it was 5.7 billion and by 1936, at 9 billion marks, it exceeded the peak year of the 1920s. The bulk of the construction was in residential housing (28 per cent) and road construction (21 per cent). The linkages established through construction with the rest of the economy were like those generated by motorisation. Demand increased rapidly for building materials and heavy machinery, for light tools and, in the case of motor vehicles, for more specialised industrial raw materials. The employment effects were also important. In 1933 only 666,000 were employed in the construction industries; by 1936 the figure was two million. It has been calculated that over 1.1 million jobs were more or less dependent on the motor vehicle and roads by 1938 [64: *478-80*]. The stimulus provided to these particular sectors also had the advantage of prompting further investment and expansion in the private economy and rapidly generating demand for ancillary goods and services. Small businesses were helped by the increase in private housebuilding and road con-struction and private investment expanded more rapidly in both these sectors than private investment as a whole.

When government expenditure and investment is broken down in detail it becomes clear that no one sector on its own was capable of generating the growth necessary to explain the recovery (see Table XIII). If anything construction and motorisation have better claims than work-creation or rearmament. What was important was the aggregate effect of all the government's spending and demand policies taken together, attacking the recession on a broad front, rather than at one particular point. Indeed the depression in Germany had been so severe and business confidence so reduced, that the government had no choice but to undertake a large part of the activity that private initiative was unwilling to undertake. This

Table XIII
*Public Expenditure in Germany by Category 1928-38 (bn RM)**

	1928	1932	1933	1934	1935	1936	1937	1938
Total expenditure (central and local)	23.2	17.1	18.4	21.6	21.9	23.6	26.9	37.1
Construction	2.7	0.9	1.7	3.5	4.9	5.4	6.1	7.9
Rearmament	0.7	0.7	1.8	3.0	5.4	10.2	10.9	17.2
Transportation +	2.6	0.8	1.3	1.8	2.1	2.4	2.7	3.8
Work creation	–	0.2	1.5	2.5	0.8	–	–	–

* There is some overlap between the categories. Work-creation included some expenditure on roads; construction also includes some rearmament expenditure.
+ Figures for national expenditure on roads and waterways. Local expenditure averaged 0.6-0.8 bn RM from 1933-5.
Source: [3: *245;* 64: *83,477;* 65: *113;* 71: *197*].

50

required the government, as Erbe has argued, to control and monitor the secondary effects of spending policies as well [22: *161-2*; 77: *972-4*]. The Nazis did not simply pump money into the economy and wait for income to be generated by others. They used the spending policies as a lever to gain greater control over other areas of the economy. In the long run this helped to divert the economy to war purposes when the time came, and it also fitted in with the Nazis' own desire to control from above, to reduce the autonomy of the market and to produce an economy sensitive to the needs of the 'people'.

Thus government spending policies, although central to the explanation of the recovery, made necessary the extension of controls over the whole economy in order to make the system work. This was recognised by economic experts like Schacht as well as by the Nazis. Under the unusual political and economic circumstances of the early 1930s, the Nazis and their economic managers argued for a 'package' of policies that would allow them to regulate economic growth as a whole. The system could only be made to work with the addition of other controls, although they never quite amounted to a central economic plan. The most important of these additional controls were over prices and wages, and over foreign trade, which was closely related. These were both areas that had an important influence on the currency, and Schacht, among others, was anxious to defend the currency and avoid inflation during the post-depression years as he had done during the 1920s. The controls over prices and wages helped to give the government's monetary policy a veneer of conservatism during the recovery period to compensate for unorthodox methods of financing. The controls over wages had another purpose as well. Wages were kept low, well below the real level of 1929–31, in the first years of recovery to give incentive to businessmen to expand business again with reduced labour costs. Unit labour costs, as Phelps Brown has shown, did not reach the 1929–31 level throughout the 1930s [70: *438*].

The controls over foreign trade and foreign exchange, which had begun in 1931, were extended by the legislation arising out of Schacht's New Plan published in 1934. Here the purpose was to prevent government spending from being used to suck in imports which the country could ill afford to pay for. The collapse of world trade made it difficult to export goods, as did the deliberate overvaluation of the mark. In the face of overwhelming protectionism abroad and the closing of some traditional export markets in the

United States and western Europe, it could be argued that Germany had little choice. In fact the control over trade matched the autarkic views of the agrarian and business supporters of the Nazi regime. Imports were to be substituted by domestic production, and the only trade allowed was in essential raw materials and foodstuffs that could not be produced at home. Much of this trade was carried on through bilateral barter agreements through which special clearing arrangements could be made to avoid pressure on the balance of payments and Germany's very small stock of gold and foreign exchange. Germany had such agreements with twenty-five countries by 1938 [61: *391-2*]. Such a policy effectively insulated the German economy against the effects of the world economy and avoided the international political and economic problems of the Weimar and depression period. But it also limited the growth of trade on which higher German economic growth depended.

Finally the government came to extend control over most of the remaining areas of the economy. These were predominantly of a supervisory rather than executive nature. Industry and trade were compelled to establish a network of territorial and industry-wide groups and chambers, although big business in particular needed little encouragement to complete a process of widespread cartelisation that had begun before the first world war and which was now designed to protect industrial interests in a period of economic and political uncertainty. Agriculture was also organised under the Reich Food Estate. Small businesses were supervised by the Chamber of Handicrafts. Banking, while fully restored to private ownership, became effectively an instrument of government policy. The capital market could only carry out those functions permitted by the state and all transactions were subject to approval. In this way the Nazi leadership was able to build up a structure of supervision that could be used at a later date for converting the economy more fully to war purposes, while it allowed those in charge of the recovery policies in the 1933–6 period to make sure that none of the variables at work in the German economy would undermine the effectiveness of the overall strategy.

Was this strategy Keynesian? Superficially, perhaps. But it is important to remember the differences. Keynes believed that expansionary policies required a low rate of interest: Schacht kept interest rates high throughout the early recovery period. Keynes argued that the marginal propensity to consume should be encouraged, and saving discouraged. In Germany the reverse happened. The same holds good for a prices and a wages policy neither of which Keynes regarded as important under conditions of less than full employment. Keynes expected state expenditure to be used to push private enterprise along the road to recovery, and that private initiative would then take over. In Germany the state chose to control and regulate the secondary effects of spending policies as well in order to turn the economy in the direction favoured by the government. Finally Keynes hoped that such expansionary policies would be linked to a renewed expansion into the world economy and a large increase in private consumption. Neither occurred under Nazism [22: *169–77*; 42: *9–24*]. If a high level of state expenditure and of government control over the economy is a sufficient definition of Keynesianism then both Hitler and Stalin can be counted among its first practitioners. The evidence suggests, however, that in terms of both the letter and the spirit of the theory the German economic recovery was not Keynesian. It was instead the product of a wide range of increasingly coercive economic policies centred around government spending to revive investment, control demand and prepare for war.

5 *State, Industry and Labour*

AGAINST the background of government recovery policies the German economy continued to modernise itself under the impact of 'technological momentum'. That is, firms continued to innovate; to adopt new production methods; to devise new products; to break down the older ways of business and replace them with modern ones. The most noticeable shifts over the recovery period occurred in the continuing process of amalgamation and the elimination of the smaller marginal producers. This was nothing peculiar to the Nazi period. Levy had charted its progress through the 1920s in his book on *Industrial Germany* published in 1935 [48]. During the 1930s some 300,000 small businesses disappeared, while cartelisation became compulsory in those areas not already cartelised. High growth occurred in the new areas of the economy, in the motor industry, in chemicals, in the aircraft industry, in electrification. The more traditional goods, including foodstuffs and textiles, recovered only slowly and continued to decline as a proportion of German industrial output as they did in the other major industrial economies (see Table XIV). The pattern of investment reflected this. The heavy industrial sector expanded almost 200 per cent over the period 1932 to 1938; the consumer industries by only 38 per cent. Industrial investment was provided by the state and by funds produced within the firms themselves on the basis of expanding profits and a fall in costs, particularly of building, labour and raw materials.

To some extent the Nazi recovery owed its success to the normal development of technical and organisational change. Indeed it is tempting to see German growth during the 1930s, as Landes has done, as the product of an increased level of technological change based around industries important for rearmament [47: *419–51*]. Yet for all these signs of change, the structural shifts were not as great during the period as they had been before 1929 or after 1945. Although there were technical and organisational changes they were not sustained enough either to cause major structural shifts in the economy or to explain the revival after 1932. If the productivity

Table XIV

Index of Production for Selected German Industries 1932–8

(1928 = 100)

	1932	1933	1935	1938
Coal	69.4	72.7	94.8	123.0
Pig iron	33.3	44.5	108.8	154.3
Steel	39.3	52.2	112.6	162.2
Motor-cars	28.6	59.7	136.1	200.7
Commercial vehicles	22.9	40.7	121.7	200.7
Electrical energy	76.5	83.7	116.3	175.9
Machinery (on order)	32.8	39.1	111.8	166.7
Chemicals	50.9	58.5	79.5	127.0
Shoes	85.3	101.5	101.7	118.5
Textiles	79.2	90.5	91.0	107.5
Household goods, Furniture	69.6	70.5	80.4	113.6

Source: [50: *46*], *Statistisches Jahrbuch für das Deutsche Reich 1938* (Berlin, 1939).

growth of the period is put into perspective it becomes clear that technical change or changes in organisation and work methods did not play as important a part in helping recovery as they did during the 1920s and 1950s. According to Rostas productivity grew only 1.3 per cent per annum during the 1929–38 period, despite the fact that the high unemployment levels of the years 1930–4 gave an involuntary boost to productivity figures [74]. Over the period 1929 to 1936 productivity in Britain rose by 2.5 per cent per annum. During the 1950s productivity in Germany grew at the rate of 4.7 per cent each year.

Given the high priority accorded to investment by the government it is surprising that the productive performance of the economy was not higher. In fact the absence of a high enough level of technological and organisational change may well explain the relatively modest multiplier impact in the 1930s already noted, and the comparatively inefficient performance of the German war economy that so surprised the British and American intelligence officers when they surveyed German industry at the end of the war. There are a number of explanations. Much of the improvement in German industry was made in the 1920s in the 'rationalisation drive'. From 1929 onwards many large firms had considerable over-capacity and cut back heavily on investment. After 1932 there was little incentive to take up the task of modernisation again and the recovery was undertaken in many cases with plant and equipment installed before the depression. Firms were reluctant to have their fingers burned twice by investing heavily in a boom that might well peter out as had that of 1927–9. There was at the same time an insufficient demand pull to encourage firms, particularly in the newer industries, fully to adopt modern factory methods. Although the car industry expanded its productive performance rapidly, output per head in American car factories was still four times as great. The radio industry was similarly well behind that of America and Britain. The pattern of the recovery itself affected the productive performance of the economy. Many of the projects were labour-intensive, and the construction industry, which grew faster than many others, was particularly so.

Nor did government policies help to raise the level of efficiency. Firms were given government subsidies to take on additional workers. Many government contracts went to firms producing expensive and advanced equipment, such as aircraft, which were not particularly efficient users of either labour or capital. This fact reflected a more general problem. Because the state assumed increasing responsibility for the economy, and for large areas of investment in particular, the normal market pressures for improving efficiency and for innovating were often lacking. Instead it became necessary for the state itself to encourage a higher level of administrative and technical efficiency and this it seems to have been either unwilling or unable to achieve [14; 79]. Part of the explanation for this lies in the lack of detailed central planning. There was a plethora of controls but little predictive planning of output, or planning designed specifically to improve productive performance. Many firms complained of the stifling effect of government controls and bureaucracy and the lack of any clear division of responsibility. This growing bureaucratisation of the economy was not compensated for by any real effort to control what actually happened on the factory floor, despite the propaganda campaigns for more rationalisation. Instead the state provided contracts on a fixed cost-plus basis, encouraging firms to produce a high-priced end product at the expense of the taxpayer. High profits could be made out of safe government orders. It became less necessary for German firms to be competitive and productivity suffered accordingly.

Much of what industry did in the 1930s was determined not so much by economic considerations as by political circumstances. Mason has convincingly argued that the Third Reich saw the 'primacy of politics' in the economy [55]. Entrepreneurs were no longer in a position to make judgements that were independent of the political framework within which they were compelled to operate. To many historians this has seemed quite natural. The Nazi regime was put into power by big business to oppress labour and raise profits. Turner has questioned the first of these assumptions. Some big businessmen did contribute to the Nazi election funds but German capitalism cannot be regarded, on the evidence, as having collectively brought fascism to power in any direct sense [90]. Fascism in Germany was a mass movement brought to power through collusion with a bankrupt but traditional élite, not as the puppet of big business. If German capitalism bears any responsibility for the victory of Nazism it lies, as Nolte and Weisbrod have argued, in the failure of capitalism, and heavy industry in particular, to make the democratic regime work better, rather than in any positive desire to be governed by Nazis [63; 91].

It is of course true that there were areas where the interests of Nazism and big business appeared to coincide. Profits did rise under the Third Reich, though they were closely controlled. Not enough is yet known about profitability and industrial policy to say more [87]. Labour was oppressed and wages controlled. Schacht and other bankers and businessmen were given responsibility for the first three years of recovery and Hitler allowed them a considerable degree of autonomy in economic affairs. The Nazis accepted this because they needed recovery. But against this has to be set the fact that confidence in the private economy did not revive as it had done in the 1920s. Many businessmen were wary of long-term plans in case the boom petered out or the Nazis embarked on adventurism at home or abroad. There also existed very different interests among the various groups that made up German industry. These interests had become explicit in the arguments over policy during the depression. The divisions were still there during the Third Reich. Export-orientated firms demanded a higher level of trade throughout the 1930s but failed to get it. The manufacturers of consumer goods were at a permanent disadvantage in terms of investment and sales throughout the 1930s. For them low wages and government restrictions were the opposite of their economic interests. Even heavy industry, that had favoured some degree of autarky and state aid in the early 1930s, found that the extent of state control exercised after 1936, and the rise of a state-owned industrial sector, threatened their interests too. The strains that such a relationship produced have already been demonstrated for the car industry, the aircraft industry and the iron and steel industry; but much more research is needed to arrive at a satisfactory historical judgement of the relationship between Nazism and German business. What is already clear is that the Third Reich was not simply a businessman's regime underpinning an authoritarian capitalism but on the contrary that it set about reducing the autonomy of the economic élite and subordinating it to the interests of the Nazi state.

Over all the internal divisions within industry stood the authority and interests of the Nazi movement itself. Industry was subordinate to the requirements of the party. Control over the whole economy passed into the state's hands during the political crisis of 1936–7 and the establishment of the Four Year Plan, an economic programme to increase war production and production of synthetic substitutes for vital raw materials [16: *49–65;* 81] By 1936 Hitler was determined to wage war and the economy was needed to serve military purposes. Some businesses flourished under the state, but many of them were state-owned or had become, like I.G. Farben (the large chemical combine), so penetrated by Nazi sympathisers and government funds as to be indistinguishable from firms directly owned. One result of the growing control over the economy was the development of 'defensive' strategies, particularly by big business, to safeguard the interests of the private owners or shareholders and to divert Nazi policies towards those more favourable to industry. Here the cartel organisation proved useful to industry. Firms fell back on the technical expertise embodied in the cartel organisation to argue against policies on technical grounds, and used the solidarity of the cartel to obstruct the efforts of Nazi bureaucrats. When they could industries ignored political instructions until compelled to accept them under the threat of force. In this way the iron and steel producers were able to sabotage efforts to use low-grade iron ores for three or four years, and car producers to hold up the development of the *Volkswagen* for three years, until the state took both projects over. Another defence was to use government subsidies, loopholes in the tax laws and loosely worded contracts to accumulate hidden reserves that were used to strengthen corporate power at the expense of government investment policy [50: *126*]. The ambivalent attitude of business to the Nazi regime finally took the form in 1938–9 of a further, though much subdued, debate on economic strategy like the debate during the depression [80: *167–72*]. As in 1931 the government refused to listen to the alternatives.

The fact that businessmen were compelled to operate in a political sphere over which they had less and less influence affected economic performance accordingly. By contrast the more favourable climate of the 1950s encouraged businessmen to take an active and influential part in developing a buoyant consumer-orientated economy. The same was true for labour. After 1933 government policy was directed towards keeping wages low and removing all independent labour organisations that could argue for better pay or conditions. Trade unions were closed down on 1 May 1933, and many union leaders imprisoned. The unions were replaced by a corporate institution, the Nazi Labour Front, which was made up of all employers and employees; but with labour legislation strongly favouring the employers the new spirit of 'co-operation' in labour relations was more nominal than real. In each factory Nazi Trustees of Labour were appointed by the Labour Front to act as agents between the authorities and the workforce. Strikes were outlawed and penalties for any kind of industrial action were severe. Nazi attempts to sugar the pill with the 'Strength through Joy' holiday and leisure organisation or the 'Beauty of Work' movement for decorating factories prettily have been shown to be simply cosmetic and a poor substitute for free bargaining [54; 72].

If employment levels were significantly raised it was at the expense of any real increase in earnings or improvements in standards of living, both of which the government deliberately chose to restrain in order to divert money and resources to war. Nathan has shown that the consumption of a range of important foodstuffs by working-class German families declined between 1927 and 1937 and that those that increased tended to be in poorer substitutes, such as potatoes and rye-bread (see Table XV). Salary earners did better, though not much better, when account is taken of higher tax payments and compulsory levies.

The effect of labour policies on economic performance is hard to judge quantitatively. The overall structure of the labour market changed very little over the period. Labour input rose only slowly in the inter-war period in comparison with the pre-1914 and post-1945 economies. There was a very slight movement from the land to the towns, but a corresponding movement the other way as the Nazis attempted to revitalise rural life. Much labour was absorbed into low-paid work-creation schemes, into the Labour Service (compulsory conscription of young people for community projects) or into the armed forces. All these diversions affected aggregate demand and overall growth not only because they were to areas of poor productive

Table XV

Consumption in Working-Class Families 1927 and 1937 (annual)*

	1927	1937	% change
Rye bread (kg)	262.9	316.1	+ 20.2
Wheat bread (kg)	55.2	30.8	– 44.2
Meat and meat products (kg)	133.7	109.2	– 18.3
Bacon (kg)	9.5	8.5	– 10.5
Milk (ltr)	427.8	367.2	– 14.2
Cheese (kg)	13.0	14.5	+ 11.5
Eggs (number)	404	237	– 41.3
Fish (kg)	21.8	20.4	– 6.4
Vegetables (kg)	117.2	109.6	– 6.5
Potatoes (kg)	499.5	519.8	+ 4.1
Sugar (kg)	47.2	45.0	– 4.7
Tropical fruit (kg)	9.7	6.1	– 37.1
Beer (ltr)	76.5	31.6	– 58.7

*Adjusted for changes in purchasing-power and family size. Includes family
budgets of low-paid civil servants and salaried workers.
Source: [60: *358*].

use and low incomes, but because the labour was denied to those
industries that needed it when full employment returned, and which
would have used it more productively. There was also the problem of
mobilising female labour. Although it is a myth that female
employment fell during the Third Reich because the Nazis wanted
women to return to home and kitchen, it did not expand either,
denying German industry access to a large labour reserve and
reducing the chances of expanding growth by accelerating labour
input. Long has calculated that both before and during the war the
German economy made less efficient use of its labour resources than
Britain or the United States [49: *16–18*]. To some extent this is
understandable. If labour did not openly resist Nazi labour policies, it
did not co-operate either. Like industry, labour adopted defensive
tactics in the face of the political and economic threat from the Nazi
party. Veiled strikes, absenteeism, a reluctance to participate in the
introduction of new factory methods, a prolonged defence of traditional skills and demarcation all contributed to the less efficient
utilisation of labour [54].

6   Full Employment and the Coming of War

IN discussing economic recovery the historian should ask not only *why* it happened, but also what was the recovery *for?* In most cases the answer is economic – higher profits, sustained economic growth, higher living standards. In the case of the German recovery in the 1930s the answer was German imperialism and war. Historians disagree about what kind of war it was supposed to be, or the extent to which the economy was actually prepared for war, but there is no disagreement that the German economy was being prepared for some degree of military expansion.

What primarily concerns us here is not the course of diplomacy or German strategy but the effect of war preparation on economic growth. To understand this impact it is necessary to divide the period into two parts. From 1932 to 1936 the priority of the government was to achieve recovery through a combination of demand and investment policies. Rearmament was only a small part of the strategy. From 1936 to 1939, that is during the period of full employment, the priority switched to war preparation. The change in economic strategy was signalled by the second Four Year Plan set up in October 1936, which gave Göring responsibility for reorientating the economy for war and achieving self-sufficiency in essential war materials – oil, rubber and steel. During the second period it became necessary for the government to achieve control over all investment and trade to ensure that the economy moved in the directions necessary for war. It was also necessary to restrict the growth of private consumption in favour of state expenditure for military and economic preparations. 'The economy', Göring declared, 'must be completely converted for war.' In 1937/8 military expenditure increased to 10 billion marks, in 1938/9 to 17 billion, or 17 per cent of GNP. In addition much of the public investment that was not directly military was used for synthetic or substitute production whose purpose was to increase Germany's ability to wage war. When compared with any other major industrial power the proportion of the German economy geared to war was very significant.

It was during the period of growing war preparation that the limits of the German economic recovery were shown. It has already been pointed out that by any long-term measurement the achievement of the 1930s was not very remarkable. Even by 1937 the economy was only just above the level reached some twenty-five years before. From 1936 onwards all the indices of growth began to slow down. If the short-term recovery had been achieved with remarkable speed, the longer-term prospects for growth were much more muted. The switch to war preparation did not produce any real crisis in the economy before September 1939 but it did increasingly compromise the achievements already made.

One problem was finance. During 1938 the money supply grew much faster than output, 22 per cent against only 4 per cent growth in industrial output. The government's desire to increase war expenditure led to a continued expansion of the Reich debt and a growing diversion of resources away from the consumer sector. The competition for resources under conditions of full employment, rising world prices and raw material scarcity led to a veiled inflation that was only repressed by the government's strict enforcement of wage and price controls. The inflation itself might well have acted as a mild stimulus to growth had it not been for the fact that it stemmed from non-productive military expenditure and not from a rapid rise in consumer spending. Nor would it have mattered so much if output per man-hour had been expanding buoyantly, but that, too, was not the case.

Another problem was demand. After 1936 the government was anxious to cut the unrestricted growth of consumer demand in favour of war preparations. The slowing down of the growth of consumption affected overall economic growth and hence the ability of the economy to support the high levels of arms spending. Industrialists wanted the opposite to happen – more home demand, particularly for durables, and an expansion of exports to encourage high growth and technical change in the consumer industries. The Nazis did not want this. Instead it has been shown that they deliberately increased the marginal propensity to save and discouraged the growth of consumption. It was this switch to relatively less productive military expenditures that slowed up economic growth after 1936/7. In fact it was at just the point where the government spending policies might have been expected to stimulate a sharp upswing in private business activity along Keynesian lines that the government chose to control that activity and divert much of it to war. The government moved, in

Schumpeter's words, from 'additive' to 'substitutive' spending; from adding new resources to using resources that would otherwise have been taken up by private industry in a different way [77: *ii, 974*].

Some of these problems would have mattered less if the war industries had themselves been efficient and military expenditure been disbursed to encourage growth. But for a number of reasons they were not. Carroll has argued that it was administrative inefficiency that made rearmament industrially inefficient. Other historians have emphasised the structural problems: confused planning, labour shortages, poor factory organisation, excessive military interference [17; 57; 66]. One major problem was the amount of money spent on organising and administering military life instead of spending more on weapons and industrial investment to produce them. Another problem was the amount of sheer financial waste produced by incompetent military or bureaucratic authorities with insufficient experience of industrial and management questions. Below these groups were industrialists either demoralised by the direction that Nazi policy was taking or happy to produce inefficiently at the government's and taxpayers' expense. No doubt all these factors contributed to the relatively poor growth effect that rearmament and war preparation produced.

It could indeed be argued that one of the factors that allowed the economy to grow as much as it did during the 1936–9 period was the ability of the consumer sector to divert or ignore Nazi policies on war preparation and to continue to press for a growth of consumer demand. Many firms could count on the incompetence or inertia of the state supervisory offices to get around the problem of controls. The car industry struggled to export more during 1938 and 1939, and continued to absorb large quantities of rubber and fuel that the army authorities wanted to stockpile. When war broke out in 1939 the motor industry was still without a full mobilisation plan and had been able to resist almost all plans for its enforced rationalisation for war purposes. But growth limits operated for the car industry too, and output in 1938 and 1939 was only marginally above the levels achieved in 1937.

It is important to remember that there were limits to growth under the Nazi regime, and that rearmament on a large scale did restrict further economic expansion. It is tempting to ask at this point whether the economy could not have grown faster if the government had persisted with demand and recovery policies and had not switched to war preparation. Most economists are agreed that it could have grown faster if trade and consumer demand had been allowed to develop with their own momentum out of the early government-created recovery [22: *ch. 8*; 53: *185-9*]. For the historian this is of course speculation, not history; but it is difficult not to agree on the evidence of the *Wirtschaftswunder* of the post-war years, that there are more appropriate and less painful strategies for growth than that adopted in the 1930s.

7 *Conclusion*

THE debate on the German inter-war economy has not yet been completed but enough work has been done to fill in the important answers. More research is needed on the relationship between industry and government in the 1930s, and on questions to do with profitability and productivity. But on many aspects of the period it is possible to reach more definite conclusions.

The problems of economic growth during the inter-war years were nowhere so acute as in Germany. The structural problems of the world economy in the 1920s were exaggerated in their effect upon Germany because of the results of the war and inflation. These problems had already led to a downturn of business activity before the world slump occurred. The subsequent depression was then intensified by the fall in foreign lending and by government deflationary policies which were pursued partly because the unorthodox alternatives were unacceptable, but largely because of internal and external political constraints. It was the combination of such constraints and the structural problems of the economy that forced the business cycle downwards to the point where many Germans were prepared to accept more radical alternatives, both Communist and National Socialist.

The triumph of the Nazi alternative in 1933 led to the rapid intro-duction of a wide range of government policies designed to augment and speed up the existing recovery. Particular emphasis was put on investment-led growth and on public expenditure and fiscal conces-sions designed to expand demand. Before 1936 the bulk of expendi-ture was on work-creation, motorisation and general construction. After 1936 rearmament became increasingly important. Throughout the 1933–9 period the government continued to extend the range of controls and to substitute public for private activity in order to pursue the political aims of the regime.

Did these controls amount to a fascist economic system? If the controls are looked at in isolation it can be seen that many, with the exception of the stringent labour laws, have been used to a greater or lesser extent by liberal western economies since the war. Many of the Nazi policies had their roots in the Weimar period too. The important thing to emphasise is that the controls and policies cannot be viewed on their own. If the policy instruments that the Nazis used have become conventional instruments by twentieth-century standards, the objectives of policy have not. It is impossible to view Nazi policies for the economy in isolation. They form a unit inseparable in the end from the political and ideological purposes of the regime. It is the political ends, the repression of labour, the controls over business, the plans for war, the social programme, that distinguish the Nazi regime from its liberal successors. The Nazi 'economic system' became simply a part of the Nazi 'political' system, closer in character to the economy of Stalin's Russia than to those of the capitalist west.

Nevertheless German capitalism survived the experience of Nazism. The process of economic modernisation, if it owed little directly to the Nazis, was not reversed during the 1930s. Hitler tempered ideology with pragmatism, controlling but not transforming the economy as in Russia. Moreover business itself found ways of diverting the full impact of the regime. The difficulties experienced in converting the economy for war were due to some extent to the inefficient Nazi administrative machine faced with a defensive and strongly cartelised industrial structure. There were limits to the extent that the Nazis could divert the recovered economy to war purposes. Indeed what efforts were made to create an economy for waging war had the effect of slowing down recovery and growth, stifling initiative and creating business uncertainty once again. 'Recovery' in this context was a dead end.

Select Bibliography

THE following list is by no means exhaustive. It includes most of works in English which deal with important aspects of the debates on the German economy. There are also a number of books and articles in German, which have been included where there is no ready English alternative or where the item is of particular importance. Comments have been added to most references to explain as briefly as possible the author's contribution to the discussion.

[1]   D. Abraham, *The Collapse of the Weimar Republic* (1981).

[2]   D. Aldcroft, *The European Economy 1914–70* (1978). A brief but useful survey, placing weight on explanations other than rearmament for the upswing before 1936.

[3]   S. Andic and J. Veverka, 'The Growth of Government Expenditure in Germany since the Unification', *Finanzarchiv*, XXIII (1964).

[4]   H. Arndt, *Economic Lessons of the Nineteen-Thirties* (1944).

[5]   F. Baerwald, 'How Germany Reduced Unemployment', *American Economic Review*, XXIV (1934). A useful discussion of the impact of recovery policies on different industries.

[6]   T. Balderston, 'The German Business Cycle in the 1920s: a Comment', *Economic History Review*, 2nd ser., XXX (1977).

[7]   T. Balogh, 'The National Economy of Germany', *Economic Journal*, XLVIII (1938). A pioneering discussion of the Nazi economy, placing much emphasis on rearmament to explain its growth and structure.

[8]   A. L. Baster, 'Some Economic Aspects of Rearmament', *International Labour Review*, XXXVII (1938).

[9]   E. Bennett, *Germany and the Diplomacy of the Financial Crisis, 1931* (1962).

[10] R. Bessell, 'Eastern Germany as a Structural Problem in the Weimar Republic', *Social History*, III (1978).

[11] K. Borchardt, 'Zwangslagen und Handlungsspielräume in der grossen Wirtschaftskrise der frühen dreissiger Jahre', *Jahrbuch*

der Bayerischen Akademie der Wissenschaften (1979). An important reinterpretation of the Brüning era, stressing the theoretical and political constraints operating on government economic policy, and the lack of a realistic alternative.

[12] R. A. Brady, *Business as a System of Power* (1943). Argues that the German economy of the 1930s was the logical outcome of the developing expansionism of German big business.

[13] _____, *The Rationalization Movement in German Industry* (1933).

[14] C. Bresciani-Turroni, 'The Multiplier in Practice', *Review of Economic Statistics*, xx (1938).

[15] G. Bry, *Wages in Germany 1871–1945* (1960). Provides a full statistical survey on German wages and earnings over the period.

[16] W. Carr, *Arms, Autarky and Aggression* (1972). Emphasises the importance of political and ideological influences on economic policy under Hitler.

[17] B. A. Carroll, *Design for Total War: Arms and Economics in the Third Reich* (1968). A study of military spending and its place in the German economy in the late 1930s. Emphasises the administrative inefficiency of the military–economic structure.

[18] F. Child, *The Theory and Practice of Exchange Control in Germany* (1958).

[19] W. Conze (ed.), *Die Staats-und Wirtschaftskrise des Deutschen Reiches* (1967). Contains useful essays on the depression period, particularly by D. Keese on growth in the economy.

[20] J. S. Davis, *The World between the Wars, 1919–39: an Economist's View* (1975). Blames the crisis in Germany on the withdrawal of short-term United States lending.

[21] H. S. Ellis, *Exchange Control in Central Europe* (1941).

[22] R. Erbe, *Die nationalsozialistische Wirtschaftspolitik 1933–9 im Lichte der modernen Theorie* (1958). An important contribution to the debate on economic recovery. Emphasises rearmament as a key to growth, and examines the economy from a Keynesian viewpoint. Concludes that Nazi economic strategy was not Keynesian.

[23] W. Eucken, 'On the Theory of the Centrally Administered Economy: An Analysis of the German Experiment', *Economica*, xv (1948). A discussion of the growth of controls in the 1930s and the nature of Nazi planning.

[24] M. E. Falkus, 'The German Business Cycle in the 1920s', *Economic History Review*, 2nd ser., XXVIII (1975). Argues that foreign lending was crucial in explaining the course of business activity in Germany, rather than a domestically induced recession.

[25] J. E. Farquharson, *The Plough and the Swastika: The NSDAP and Agriculture in Germany 1928–1945* (1976). Goes some way towards filling the gap of the role of agriculture in German economic growth.

[26] G. D. Feldman, 'The Social and Economic Policies of German Big Business 1918–1929', *American Historical Review*, LXXV (1969).

[27] W. Fischer and P. Czada, 'Wandlungen in der deutschen Industriestruktur im 20 Jahrhundert', in G. Ritter (ed.), *Entstehung und Wandel der modernen Gesellschaft* (1970). An important long-term view of the structural changes in the German economy.

[28] H. Fleisig, 'War-Related Debts and the Great Depression', *American Economic Review* (Papers and Proceedings), LXVI (1976). Argues that withdrawal or reduction of United States funds caused depression, together with effect of fall in United States imports. Stresses work-creation in Nazi recovery.

[29] J. A. Garraty, 'The New Deal, National Socialism and the Great Depression', *American Historical Review*, LXXVIII (1973). Somewhat unconvincing comparison of Nazi and New Deal economic and social policies.

[30] G. Garvy, 'Keynes and the Economic Activists of Pre-Hitler Germany', *Journal of Political Economy*, LXXXIII (1975). Shows that Keynesian theory had been anticipated in German theoretical discussion before and during the depression.

[31] D. Gessner, 'Agrarian Protectionism in the Weimar Republic', *Journal of Contemporary History*, XII (1977). A useful discussion of a major aspect of 'interest-group' politics.

[32] L. Grebler, 'Work-Creation Policy in Germany 1932–5', Parts I and II, *International Labour Review*, XXXV (1937).

[33] D. Guerin, *Fascism and Big Business* (1939).

[34] C. Guillebaud, *The Economic Recovery of Germany 1933–38* (1939). Unpopular at the time of publication, the book was the first serious academic discussion of German recovery policies. Puts rearmament in perspective and emphasises the wide

number of instruments used for economic regulation.

[35] G. Hallgarten, 'Adolf Hitler and German Heavy Industry, 1931–33', *Journal of Economic History*, XII (1952). Argues that big business had an important part to play in securing Hitler's rise to power.

[36] J. L. Heinemann, 'Count von Neurath and German Policy at the London Economic Conference, 1933', *Journal of Modern History*, XXXI (1969).

[37] W. Hoffmann, *Das Wachstum der deutschen Wirtschaft seit der Mitte des 19 Jahrhunderts* (1965). Essential statistical analysis of German economic growth.

[38] K. Holl (ed.), *Wirtschaftskrise und liberale Demokratie* (1978). Contains a useful article by Feldman on industrial policy during the depression.

[39] T. Hughes, 'Technological Momentum in History: Hydrogenation in Germany 1898–1933', *Past & Present*, XV (1969).

[40] H. James, 'State, Industry and Depression in Weimar Germany', *Historical Journal*, XXIV (1981).

[41] D. E. Kaiser, *Economic Diplomacy and the Origins of the Second World War: Germany, Britain, France, and Eastern Europe 1930–1939* (1980).

[42] J. M. Keynes, *The Means to Prosperity* (1933).

[43] C. Kindleberger, *The World in Depression 1929–1939* (1973). Stresses the role of short-term lending in explaining the severity of the German collapse. Less useful on the recovery period.

[44] B. H. Klein, *Germany's Economic Preparations for War* (1959). Argues that rearmament was not important until at least 1936/7 and that its economic impact thereafter has been exaggerated.

[45] J. J. Klein, 'German Money and Prices', in M. Friedman (ed.), *Studies in the Quantity Theory of Money* (1956).

[46] J. Kuczynski, *Germany. Economic and Labour Conditions under Fascism* (1945).

[47] D. Landes, *The Unbound Prometheus* (1970). Stresses the role of United States lending in explaining the German depression. Less useful for the recovery but an interesting analysis of the late 1930s and the inefficiency of the military economy.

[48] H. Levy, *Industrial Germany* (1935).

[49] C. D. Long, *The Labor Force under Changing Income and Employment* (1958).

[50] S. Lurie, *Private Investment in a Controlled Economy: Germany 1933–1939* (1947). An important guide to Nazi investment

policy and the changes in the private capital market.

[51] A. Maddison, *Economic Growth in the West* (1964). An essential general discussion of growth, putting the Nazi recovery in perspective.

[52] _____, 'Growth and Fluctuation in the World Economy 1870–1960', *Banca Nazionale del Lavoro Quarterly* (Sept. 1972).

[53] K. Mandelbaum, 'An Experiment in Full Employment: Controls in the German Economy, 1933–8' in Oxford University Institute of Statistics, *The Economics of Full Employment* (1944). Argues that economic growth could have been higher in the 1930s.

[54] T. W. Mason, 'Labour in the Third Reich, 1933–1939', *Past & Present*, XII (1966). Discusses Nazi labour policy and forms of labour resistance.

[55] _____, 'The Primacy of Politics – Politics and Economics in National Socialist Germany' in S. Woolf (ed.), *The Nature of Fascism* (1968). A useful discussion of the relationship between German capitalism and German fascism.

[56] S. Merlin, 'Trends in German Economic Control since 1933', *Quarterly Journal of Economics*, LVII (1943).

[57] A. S. Milward, *The German Economy at War* (1965). The best discussion to date of the German war economy. Stresses the limited role of arms in the economy before 1941.

[58] E. B. Mittelman, 'The German Use of Unemployment Insurance Funds for Works Purposes', *Journal of Political Economy*, XLVI (1938).

[59] H. Mommsen, D. Petzina and B. Weisbrod (eds), *Industrielles System und politische Entwicklung in der Weimarer Republik* (1974). The proceedings of a major conference with useful papers by Fischer, Petzina, Milward and Weisbrod.

[60] O. Nathan and M. Fried, *The Nazi Economic System* (1944). A detailed study of the operation of controls under the Nazis. Emphasises that rearmament was at the expense of civilian consumption.

[61] L. Neal, 'The Economics and Finance of Bilateral Clearing Agreements: Germany 1934–8', *Economic History Review*, 2nd ser., XXXII (1979).

[62] F. Neumann, *Behemoth: The Structure and Practice of National Socialism* (1942). An important theoretical discussion; argues that the Nazi economy was a 'command economy' run on behalf of 'state monopoly capitalism'.

[63] E. Nolte, 'Big Business and German Politics: a Comment',

American Historical Review, LXXV (1969). A useful and brief summary of the debate over the responsibility of big business for the rise of Hitler. Argues that the case is not sufficiently proved.

[64] R. J. Overy, 'Cars, Roads and Economic Recovery in Germany, 1932–8', *Economic History Review*, 2nd ser., XXVIII (1975). Argues that motorisation was an important government priority in promoting recovery.

[65] _____, 'The German *Motorisierung* and Rearmament: a Reply', *Economic History Review*, 2nd ser., XXXII (1979). Contains full details on the statistics of rearmament from 1932 to 1939.

[66] _____, 'Transportation and Rearmament in the Third Reich', *Historical Journal*, XVI (1973).

[67] M. Palyi, 'Economic Foundations of the German Totalitarian State', *American Journal of Sociology*, XLVI (1941). Discusses the anti-capitalist nature of the Nazi regime.

[68] E. N. Peterson, *Hjalmar Schacht: For and Against Hitler* (1954).

[69] D. Petzina, 'Germany and the Great Depression', *Journal of Contemporary History*, IV (1969). Stresses internal rather than external political pressures on Brüning. Gives considerable weight to agriculture.

[70] E. H. Phelps Brown, *A Century of Pay* (1968). Useful figures on the long-term performance of the German economy.

[71] K. E. Poole, *German Financial Policies 1932–1939* (1939). Stresses role played in recovery by government spending. Critical of public-works programmes in the recovery.

[72] A. G. Rabinbach, 'The Aesthetics of Production in the Third Reich', *Journal of Contemporary History*, XI (1976).

[73] W. Röpke, 'Trends in German Business Cycle Policy', *Economic Journal*, XLIII (1933). Interesting detail on the alternative policies in the depression from one of the protagonists in the debate.

[74] L. Rostas, 'Industrial Production, Productivity and Distribution in Britain, Germany and the United States, 1935–7', *Economic Journal*, LIII (1943). Useful article but should be used with some caution in drawing comparisons. Figures for German productivity are, however, confirmed elsewhere.

[75] H. Schacht, *Account Settled* (1949). A rather insubstantial survey of German policy in the 1930s and Schacht's role in it. Useful in

demonstrating areas of continuity.

[76] C. T. Schmidt, *German Business Cycles 1924–1933* (1933).

[77] J. Schumpeter, *Business Cycles* (2 vols, 1939). Argues that government played a key role in sustaining the upswing, at the expense of private business and consumption. Stresses importance of the revival of agriculture and control over foreign trade and exchange.

[78] A. Schweitzer, *Big Business in the Third Reich* (1964). Major study of the Nazi economy, stressing the role of rearmament in the recovery and the role played by cartels in the political relationship between business and Nazis.

[79] _____, 'Profits under Nazi Planning', *Quarterly Journal of Economics*, LX (1946).

[80] A. E. Simpson, *Hjalmar Schacht in Perspective* (1969).

[81] _____, 'The Struggle for Control of the German Economy, 1936–7', *Journal of Modern History*, XXI (1959). Argues that there occurred a break in Nazi economic policy in 1936/7, with greater government control thereafter.

[82] A. Sohn-Rethel, *Economy and Class-Structure of German Fascism* (1978). An interesting discussion from an economist who worked in Germany during the depression. Useful for an analysis of divisions within German industry.

[83] G. Spenceley, 'R. J. Overy and the *Motorisierung*: a Comment', *Economic History Review*, 2nd ser., XXXII (1979). Argues that construction was more important than motorisation in the recovery period.

[84] D. Stegmann, B. Wendt, P-C. Witt (eds), *Industrielle Gesellschaft und politische System* (1978). Contains a useful article by Jochmann critical of Brüning's deflationary strategy.

[85] G. Stolper, *The German Economy: 1870 to the Present* (1967). Places emphasis on agriculture as an explanation for depression and during the revival. Explains recovery through public-spending policies but argues that recovery might have been greater without the Nazis.

[86] I. Svennilson, *Growth and Stagnation in the European Economy* (1954). An important general discussion of the determinants of growth in Europe between the wars. Stresses slow growth of demand due to slower population growth and the fall in trade. Argues that the role of the state was less important than in the post-war period.

[87] M. Sweezy, 'German Corporate Profits 1926–1938', *Quarterly Journal of Economics*, LIV (1940).

[88] P. Temin, 'The Beginning of the Depression in Germany', *Economic History Review*, 2nd ser., XXIV (1971). Argues that the depression was the result of domestic factors as much as foreign lending and that the downturn occurred before the fall in foreign credit.

[89] J. Theis, 'Hitler's European Building Programme', *Journal of Contemporary History*, XIII (1978).

[90] H. A. Turner, 'Big Business and the Rise of Hitler', *American Historical Review*, LXXV (1969). Argues against the thesis that big business helped to bring Hitler to power.

[91] B. Weisbrod, 'Economic Power and Political Stability Reconsidered: Heavy Industry in Weimar Germany', *Social History*, IV (1979).

[92] M. Wolfe, 'The Development of Nazi Monetary Policy', *Journal of Economic History*, XV (1955).

[93] S. Woolf, 'Did a Fascist Economic System Exist?', in Woolf (ed.), *The Nature of Fascism* (1968). Stresses importance of investment boom during the 1930s, and the spread of interdependent controls over the economy.

[94] W. S. Woytinsky, *Stormy Passage* (1961).

Index